BEING & THE BIRDS

OR: EVERYTHING YOU ALWAYS WANTED TO KNOW ABOUT HEIDEGGER (BUT WERE AFRAID TO ASK HITCHCOCK)

DEREK HAWTHORNE

Cinephile Books

2024

Cover design by Kevin I. Slaughter

Published in the United States by
CINEPHILE BOOKS

Hardcover ISBN: 978-1-64264-038-0
Paperback ISBN: 978-1-64264-039-7
E-book ISBN: 978-1-64264-040-3

CONTENTS

INTRODUCTION

The Birds is the fifty-third feature film directed by Alfred Hitchcock. Released in 1963, it is very loosely based on a 1952 short story by Daphne Du Maurier (whose *Jamaica Inn* and *Rebecca* Hitchcock had filmed in, respectively, 1939 and 1940). Instead of using an established actress, Hitchcock cast an unknown, Tippi Hedren, in the lead role. At the time, Hedren was a successful fashion model who had appeared on the covers of major magazines but had no previous acting experience. Her collaboration with Hitchcock has acquired a certain amount of notoriety in the intervening years, since Hedren has claimed that Hitchcock sexually harassed her during the making of their second film together, *Marnie* (1964).

The Birds depicts a series of savage and inexplicable bird attacks on Bodega Bay, a sleepy little California fishing village. Significantly, the attacks coincide with the arrival in town of Hedren's character, Melanie Daniels, a spoiled socialite. In this book I will take the reader through the major events of the film, and, for the cinephiles among my readers, I will include some asides about the making of *The Birds*. The secondary reason for the plot summary is to make my commentary intelligible to those who haven't seen the film, or haven't seen it in a long time. The primary reason is to present my commentary, which I do throughout. I would therefore ask those who are quite familiar with the film to read each chapter anyway, given that I believe my commentary will contain many surprises. I recommend that those who have not seen *The Birds* see it before reading this book.

I would characterize my own philosophical and political standpoint as conservative, and the book's intended audience is conservatives interested in cinema and philosophy. However, I would be quite pleased if others read and profit from it as well.

Martin Heidegger is the major influence on my commentary. I believe that Heidegger is the key to understanding this enigmatic film, which has haunted me for years. There is no evidence that Hitchcock or Evan Hunter (the screenwriter of *The Birds*) were familiar with Heidegger's philosophy. I am not claiming that Heidegger was an *influence* on the film. However, I will explore Hitchcock's own comments about the meaning of *The Birds* and argue that they lend some support to my Heideggerian interpretation.

I endorse Roland Barthes's "death of the author" thesis, which amounts to the claim that texts mean more than their authors are aware of. This is particularly true in the case of Hitchcock. His films are loaded with psychological subtext, though it is unclear if he was aware of this in all cases. Though he was a highly intelligent man with cultivated tastes, Hitchcock admitted on more than one occasion that he was an almost entirely visual thinker. He could not be described as an intellectual, and the reports of his collaborators contain no suggestion that he ever sought to deliberately inject "meaning" into his films.

Ostensibly, this book is about *The Birds*, but its greater, or larger purpose is to introduce readers to Heidegger's thought. I believe that Heidegger is, without question, the greatest philosopher since Nietzsche, and one of the greatest in history, standing shoulder to shoulder with Plato, Aristotle, Kant, Hegel, and Nietzsche—though admittedly he can also be said to stand on their shoulders (and, indeed, all these men stand on the shoulders of Plato).

But why introduce readers to Heidegger through a commentary on *The Birds*? Because *The Birds* is a genuinely gripping and mysterious film—one of the greatest works of the "master of suspense." In conjoining

Heidegger with cinema, I am able to illustrate, in relatively simple terms, some of the most difficult ideas in Heidegger's philosophy in a manner that is vivid, exciting, emotionally moving, and immediate.

Why Heidegger? Why is he one of the greats? Most of the book serves as an answer to this question. Though readers must be patient: Heidegger will not be discussed directly until Chapter Four. It is worth the wait, for I can promise the reader that Heidegger has some extraordinarily original and challenging ideas about the human condition, as well as a devastating critique of modern technological civilization and its cultural conceits.

The chapters in this book originally appeared at *Counter-Currents* but have been significantly revised since then. They were written in 2020, in the midst of the COVID-19 pandemic and during the BLM riots. I was living in New York City at the time and confined mostly to my apartment—for the simple reason that there was nowhere to go: everything except drugstores and grocery stores had been closed. BLM had come to New York, and I anxiously waited for the rioters to appear on my street. Instead, they contented themselves mainly with seeking "equity" through smashing and looting fashionable boutiques on Fifth Avenue. I was living in an unfashionable part of town and so, as it turned out, relatively safe.

During this period, I strongly identified with Melanie and the Brenner family, holed up in the farmhouse, waiting for the apocalypse. It felt like the entire world was crumbling around me, and that nothing would ever be the same. I haven't stopped feeling that way. In this book, I understand the coming of the birds to Bodega Bay as a Heideggerian "event": a sudden shift in the being or meaning of things. I felt at the time—and, again, still feel—that we may be the living witnesses to just such an "event." The "collapse" my friends and I thought was coming many years down the road may have arrived much sooner than anyone anticipated.

In facing this collapse, are there lessons to be learned from *The Birds*? Yes, there are obvious ones like the importance of resourcefulness, staying calm under fire, and courage. Oh yes, and tribalism (see chapter seven). The less obvious lessons present opportunities for self-overcoming. We are staring into the abyss. We have absolutely no idea what is coming, and whether it will entail our victory or our destruction. Will savagery be victorious? Will we lose everything we have built? I am optimistic. We need to stay in the house and fight. Eventually we may have to pile in the car and leave, driving off into the sunrise, looking for a better place. One without "birds." But we will survive.

That's my hunch. But we do not know. As I argue in this book, echoing Heidegger, we are, in large measure, not the masters of our destiny. Now more than ever we must come to terms with Heidegger's "anti-humanism" (see chapter four). We must realize that we are in the grip of forces we do not fully understand and cannot control. We can only move forward, straight into that abyss, hoping for the best, and conducting ourselves with honor.

It is terrifying. But isn't it also exciting?

I wish to thank Greg Johnson for publishing my essays, and this book, and for his helpful feedback. In particular, I must also thank my fellow cinephile Martin Lichtmesz, who offered some intelligent responses to the original versions of these chapters, including some constructive criticism. I dedicate this book to him.

Derek Hawthorne
Bodega Bay, California
October 31st, 2023

CHAPTER ONE

As the opening credits roll, the first thing we notice that is unusual about *The Birds*, and slightly disturbing, is that it has no musical score. Music occurs only twice in the film, always as played or sung by characters. The first piece is one of Debussy's *Deux arabesques*, played by Melanie Daniels on a piano, and a song, "Risseldy Rosseldy," sung by some schoolchildren in one of the film's most memorable scenes. To my knowledge, this is the first film by Hitchcock to feature no music score or theme music since his days in silent cinema. This was certainly a bold decision, but the truth is that the film features no *conventional* score. The music is, in fact, provided by the birds themselves.

Some of the bird noises in the film are genuine, but most were produced electronically by Remi Gassmann and Oskar Sala, who are credited with "Sound Production and Composition." Gassmann and Sala created the bird calls using a device called a Trautonium, which was an early electronic instrument. The Trautonium was invented in 1929 by Friedrich Trautwein in Berlin at the Rundfunkversuchstelle, the Musikhochschule's music and radio laboratory. The basic mechanism involves a resistor wire stretched over a metal plate which is pressed in order to produce sounds.

The instrument was not marketed until the early days of the Third Reich, when a small series was produced with the inevitable name "Volkstrautonium." It had been heard in films before *The Birds*, notably in Arnold Fanck's 1930 mountain film *Storm Over Mont Blanc*,[1]

---

[1] See Derek Hawthorne, "*Storm Over Mount Blanc*," Counter-Currents, August 16, 17, 19, & 22, 2011

where it provided sound effects and also features in the music score by Paul Dessau. Oskar Sala had been heavily involved in the development of the Trautonium after being introduced to Trautwein by Paul Hindemith, who would later write several short trios for three trautoniums.

That the bird calls in the film were seen by Hitchcock as music is underscored (if you will pardon the pun) by the fact that the director engaged his longtime collaborator, composer Bernard Herrmann, as "Sound Consultant." Certainly, the music "the birds" provide is far from melodic; these are not, for the most part, the sweet sounds of tweeting birdies. They are harsh and threatening—much like modern, avant-garde concert music, in fact.[2] Although Gassman and Sala's sound effects are convincing enough as bird noises, they are just ever-so-slightly fake. As I will discuss later on, the film's photographic effects have been criticized as artificial, but there is actually a quality of artificiality that pervades the entire film. From the process shots to the bright-red fake blood to the strange mixture of accents in Bodega Bay, nothing seems real except the terror conveyed by the actors, and the real sense of unease the film produces in the audience. At a subliminal level, the electronic "score" conveys this artificiality. Generally speaking, Hitchcock was uninterested in realism (*Marnie* is even less realistic in its effects, featuring obviously fake painted backdrops

---

[2] Tony Lee Moral writes that "Hitchcock wanted a more indirect and arty approach to the soundtrack." And he quotes Hitchcock saying the following: "Conventional music usually serves either as a counterpoint or a comment on whatever scene is being played. I decided to use a more abstract approach. After all, when you put music to film, it's really sound, it isn't music *per se*." See Tony Lee Moral, *The Making of Hitchcock's* The Birds (Harpenden, UK: Kamera Books, 2015), 157.

and bad process shots). In *The Birds*, however, this lack of realism may be deliberate.

The film opens with the very beautiful Miss Hedren (a typically Nordic "Hitchcock blonde") crossing the street near Union Square in San Francisco, wearing one of the two simple but elegant outfits Edith Head designed for this film. (Hedren will spend almost the entire story wearing the second outfit, a green suit.) There is a seamless transition as the camera cuts from the location shot to a studio set—the exterior of a pet shop. Just as Melanie enters, Hitchcock exits with two terriers on leashes, the director's own beloved pets. (Hitchcock liked to get his cameos out of the way early in his films, so that they wouldn't distract the audience's attention later on.) Melanie has arrived to pick up a myna bird she ordered some days prior. Only later in the film do we learn that she intends to give the bird to her Aunt Tessa, but only after teaching it a large vocabulary of dirty words. Melanie, you see, is a spoiled little rich girl (her father is part owner of a fictitious local paper) and spends much of her time planning elaborate practical jokes.

It turns out that the myna bird hasn't arrived yet, but Melanie soon finds another way to amuse herself. When the saleswoman steps out for a moment, in walks Mitch Brenner (Rod Taylor), a tall, dark, and handsome local attorney. He appears to mistake the mischievous Melanie for a shop employee, and she plays along, enjoying her deception and quite obviously attracted to Mitch. He tells Melanie that he wants to buy a pair of lovebirds as a birthday gift for his younger sister, who is about to turn eleven. The scene that unfolds is quite amusing, as it becomes apparent to Mitch, and the audience, that Melanie not only has no idea what lovebirds look like, she has no knowledge of birds at all. The tone of the scene stands in sharp contrast to the rest of the film, and if one knew nothing about what was to come, one might assume that this is a screwball comedy.

In the end, Mitch reveals that he knows exactly who Melanie is and that it is really *he* who has been pranking *her*. He had seen Melanie in court, when she answered a summons having to do with a practical joke that resulted in the smashing of a plate glass window. "I thought you might like to know what it felt like to be on the other end of a gag," he says, and walks out. Melanie is incensed and, in the peculiar logic of the female mind, now more attracted to him than ever. "Do you have any lovebirds?" she asks the saleslady, the wheels turning in her lovely, crafty head.

Melanie manages to track Mitch down and shows up at his apartment building carrying two lovebirds in a cage, looking very pleased with herself. She places the cage outside Mitch's door, along with a snarky note. But just as she is about to make her getaway a neighbor appears and tells her that Mitch has left town for the weekend. "Where did he go?" she asks. "Bodega Bay. He goes up there every weekend," replies the neighbor (played by Richard Deacon, familiar to American audiences from *The Dick Van Dyke Show*). Realizing she can't leave the birds out in the hallway for two days, Melanie decides to do something quite impetuous, that will have far-reaching consequences: she sets off in her silver convertible Aston Martin DB2/4 to make the sixty-mile journey up the coast highway to Bodega Bay.

I should mention that I myself have made the same trip. In 2003, I and two friends made a pilgrimage to Bodega Bay to visit sites from *The Birds*. I'll have more to say about how the town was utilized in the film, and how it has changed over the years, in just a moment. The footage cinematographer Robert Burks takes of Melanie driving up the coast highway is breathtaking. In one particular shot, northern California looks positively like

Switzerland. It's one of the most beautiful parts of the United States, and the only part of California where one can still enjoy something of an escape from the multicultural hell that is the rest of the state. These scenes continue the whimsical, lighthearted tone established at the beginning of the film, as the lovebirds (clearly fake in these shots) sway gently from side to side as Melanie's car screeches along the winding highway at breakneck speed.

The Bodega Bay depicted in the film is actually an amalgamation of locations from the village of Bodega Bay and the nearby town of Bodega. Some of the film's most iconic settings are really in Bodega, including the schoolhouse. A little later, a matte painting (by the great Albert Whitlock) of Hitchcock's "Bodega Bay" is utilized, giving the audience a complete picture of the director's imaginary consolidation of sites from the two towns. When Melanie arrives, her first task is to find out where Mitch lives, and what his sister's name is, since she wants to leave a birthday card along with the lovebirds. The proprietor of the local general store (who, oddly enough, speaks with a Maine accent) is able to provide the address, but can't remember the little girl's name. The intrepid Melanie thus sets off to find the local schoolteacher, who is sure to know.

The schoolteacher, whose name is Annie Hayworth, is played by Suzanne Pleshette (best known to American audiences as Emily on *The Bob Newhart Show*, which came some years later). Melanie drops by Annie's home, next to the large, late nineteenth-century schoolhouse, just as the young woman is digging in her garden. Pleshette is pretty and conveys great intelligence, but in her gardening clothes and dirty fingers she contrasts sharply with Hedren, who wears a mink coat over her green, Chanel-style suit. Annie is able to confirm that the name of the little Brenner girl is Cathy, and she also quickly intuits that Melanie has really come to see Mitch. It's clear from her manner and her insistent questions that she has an interest in Mitch herself.

It turns out that the Brenner home is a large farmhouse across the bay, where Mitch lives (on weekends, at least) with his little sister and widowed mother, Lydia. Rather than approach the house by the road, Melanie decides to rent a motorboat and cut directly across the bay. She is an odd sight, clambering into the motorboat with her mink coat and birdcage, and she's asked if she knows how to handle the thing. "Of course," she responds, and seems to mean it. Melanie skillfully maneuvers the boat across the bay toward the house then cuts the motor and watches from a safe distance to see if anyone is around. The front door opens and Lydia and Cathy appear (both of them will be properly introduced a little later). They speak to Mitch, who is hovering near the barn, then drive away in a pickup truck. When Mitch enters the barn, Melanie sees her chance. She rows the boat to the dock, ties it up, and then swiftly enters the house, birdcage dangling from one gloved hand.

For those who have experienced the film before, seeing the first appearance of the home's interior again is curiously unsettling. Here it is empty and quiet, but we know that later it will be filled with horror and violence. Melanie leaves the lovebirds in a prominent place along with a note for Cathy, then makes her escape. She rows the boat some distance from the house, and then waits and watches. Mitch emerges from the barn and enters the house—then rushes outside after finding the lovebirds. He sees the boat. He dashes back in to get a pair of binoculars, then re-emerges. Melanie slumps down in the boat, halfheartedly trying to hide. Mitch sees her through the binoculars and grins.

Were this actually a screwball comedy starring, say, Doris Day and, well, Rod Taylor (see *The Glass Bottom*

Boat, 1966), these scenes would be accompanied by un-subtle "funny" music from somebody like Frank De Vol. Without music, however, this sequence of shots is brilliantly suspenseful. Even though we don't expect anything awful to happen at this point in the film, the very *absence* of music where we would expect it creates a subtle tone of ominousness. These people and their doings are silly and frivolous. But instead of joining in their fun, vicariously, the heavy silence that surrounds them distances us from them. They seem somehow small, and their lives trivial. *Something*, we feel, is coming. Something they have completely overlooked and cannot possibly expect. And after it comes, nothing will ever be the same again.

Having spotted Melanie in the motorboat, Mitch gets in his car and sets off on the road to town, which curves around the bay. The chase is on. Melanie starts the motor (with some difficulty) and heads for the pier, watching the progress of Mitch's car the entire way. As her boat approaches its destination, Melanie sees that Mitch has beaten her: he stands on the pier waiting. At this point, Tippi adopts an exaggeratedly pert, self-satisfied expression of false innocence. She looks like she's just begging to be slapped—and the slap comes from a seagull that suddenly swoops down and viciously strikes Melanie's head before flying away.

The first time one sees this, the scene is genuinely shocking. It was shot on a soundstage, as Hitchcock liked to film all his closeups under controlled lighting. This is readily apparent to the viewer, as Hedren is backed up by a process shot, which always looks fake (even to audiences in 1963). A stuffed seagull was sent down a wire so close to Hedren's head it looks like she's been hit. Before shooting the scene, a hairdresser had sprayed Hedren's hair until it was a stiff helmet—all except one large curl which flips upward just as the gull swoops in. This was accomplished with a jet of compressed air from a tube hidden under her hair. The whole shot is quite effective, and even though the audience knows it was faked somehow it always provokes a "how did they do that?" response (not unlike the famous plane crash scene in Hitchcock's *Foreign Correspondent*, 1940).

It is from here on that the tone of the film changes dramatically. The *something* we felt was going to happen has now happened. Or, at least, we've now gotten a glimpse of it. And we know, intuitively, that this is just the beginning.

Melanie touches her gloved hand to her head and realizes that she is bleeding. Mitch is dumbfounded by the gull's behavior. "That was the damnedest thing I ever saw," he says and solicitously helps Melanie out of the boat. He is concerned by the wound on her head and guides her toward the nearby Tides Restaurant in search of first aid. Just as they are about to enter, a fisherman passes them and asks "What happened, Mitch?" "A gull hit her," Mitch responds. The fisherman is played by Mitch Zankich, the real-life owner of the Tides Restaurant. He told Hitchcock that he could use the restaurant in the film for free if he gave him a small speaking role, and if he called the town depicted in the film Bodega Bay.[3] The Tides still exists, though the original building has been replaced with a much larger structure with a bigger dining room and a gift shop selling *Birds* memorabilia. (After all these years, Bodega Bay is still dining out on *The Birds*.) I have eaten there, and can recommend the clam chowder.

When Mitch and Melanie enter, the glamorous, wounded girl reduces all the locals to staring silence. They sit at a table and Mitch requests some peroxide from the waitress. (The interior of the restaurant, by the

---

[3] See Moral, *The Making of Hitchcock's* The Birds, 86.

way, was meticulously recreated on a soundstage.) As Mitch tends to Melanie's wound, he continues verbally jousting with her, as he had done in the pet store. Rod Taylor looks a trifle too dandy in these scenes, dressed in a white, cable knit fisherman's sweater with a paisley kerchief tied around his neck. He interrogates poor Melanie drawing on all his lawyerly skill—and Mitch is a criminal lawyer, by the way. He is obviously pleased by Melanie's interest in him, and amused by her attempts to deny that he is the real reason she drove two hours to Bodega Bay. Melanie claims that she had come up for the weekend to see Annie Hayworth, and that the two of them are old school chums. "I think you came up to see me," he says cheekily. "I loathe you," she says, as if she knows she doesn't mean it, and knows that he knows.

Suddenly, in walks Mitch's mother, Lydia, who has seen Mitch's car parked outside. The screenplay describes her as "a woman in her late forties," which would mean that she must have had Mitch when she was nineteen or twenty, since he is described as "twenty-nine or thirty." Jessica Tandy, who plays Lydia, was fifty-four at the time of filming, but still looks too young to be Rod Taylor's mother (Taylor was thirty-three). We cannot help but notice that there is a slight resemblance between Lydia and Melanie, owing mainly to their hairstyles. This resemblance was exploited by the studio's publicists, who used a drawing of Tandy, hair tangled with birds, in the film poster—though almost everyone who sees the image thinks that it is Hedren.

The screenplay says of Lydia that "There is nothing agrarian-looking about her. She speaks with the quick tempo of the city dweller, and there is lively inquiry in her eyes." Tandy, who is excellent in the part, fits this description to a tee. She eyes Melanie warily, and we immediately intuit that she sees the younger woman as a threat. As we will see, the Brenner family has a rather curious Oedipal dynamic to it. Mitch announces that he has invited Melanie to dinner, and though it's clear that his mother wants nothing to do with Melanie, she has no choice but to acquiesce. "After all, you did go to the trouble of bringing me those birds," Mitch says. Lydia is puzzled by this remark and when Mitch explains about the lovebirds, her manner becomes grave. The script describes her as "understanding completely now."

This is the second woman we've encountered in Bodega Bay who is clearly hostile to Melanie, and possessive towards Mitch. The other, of course, is Annie Hayworth, whose earlier conversation with Melanie included pointed questions about where she met Mitch and how long she plans to stay in town. Indeed, the only female in the film who doesn't seem to have any designs on Mitch is his sister Cathy. Melanie tentatively accepts Mitch's invitation to dinner at seven o'clock that evening but must keep up the pretense of having to check with Annie first to see if she's got anything planned.

In fact, after parting company with Mitch and Lydia, it's to Annie's that Melanie heads, stopping on the way to buy a nightgown at the general store. A sign in Annie's window advertises a room to let, and Melanie asks her if she can have it for just one night. Annie hesitates, then agrees. She seems to be warming to Melanie, though she cannot contain her curiosity. "Did something unexpected come up?" she asks. "Yes," Melanie responds, with a tone that suggests she doesn't think it's any of her business. Just as they are about to walk into the house, a large flock of birds flies overhead. "Don't they ever stop migrating?" Annie asks, almost as if she is annoyed by the spectacle. The script describes Melanie as "watching the sky and the birds with a curiously serious expression."

When Melanie arrives at Mitch's house the family is at first nowhere to be seen. After a moment, Mitch, Lydia, and Cathy emerge from behind the chicken sheds and approach her. "We were out back looking at the chickens," Mitch explains. "Something seems to be wrong with them." Veronica Cartwright plays Cathy very exuberantly. As soon as she meets Melanie, Cathy flings her arms around her in gratitude for the lovebirds. She is supposed to be just turning eleven in the film, but is obviously older. Cartwright was thirteen at the time (indeed, Hitchcock and cast threw her a thirteenth birthday party on set).

I have already mentioned that Tandy seems too young to be Mitch's mother—and she also seems too old to be Cathy's mother. (Had Cartwright been Tandy's own child, she would have had to have given birth to her when she was thirty-nine or forty.) Then there is the oddity of the roughly nineteen-year age difference between Mitch (supposed to be twenty-nine or thirty) and Cathy (just turning eleven). All of this contributes to giving us the uneasy sense that something is just a little bit "off" about this family. Veronica Cartwright remarked years later, "Jessica, who played my mother, was 54 at the time. She was in love with her son. My brother, played by Rod Taylor, was older than me—and later journalists often thought he was my father. It set up an interesting dynamic. I knew that my brother was attracted to this lady (played by Tippi)—she was closer to my age than my mother was."[4]

As soon as they enter the house, Lydia becomes involved in a telephone conversation with the owner of the local general store, who sold her chicken feed. Hitchcock places Tandy in the foreground, and we hear the entire conversation from her end, as Mitch and Cathy bustle about in the background and Melanie gets settled. Here, Tandy teaches a master class in acting a one-sided telephone conversation. She tells the man on the other end

---

[4] See Moral, *The Making of Hitchcock's* The Birds, 135–36.

(a Mr. Brinkmeyer) that her chickens won't eat the feed. We learn that another local farmer, Dan Fawcett, has also reported that his chickens won't eat—only Fawcett bought a different brand of feed. Thoroughly puzzled, Lydia ends the conversation by suggesting that she might pay Mr. Fawcett a visit the following day.

Dinner is not depicted and instead we transition immediately to its aftermath. Melanie is seated at the piano playing one of Debussy's *Arabesques*, exactly as specified in the screenplay (and, as noted earlier, this is one of only two pieces of music heard in the entire film). She is obviously the sort of young woman who, in bygone days, was sent to "finishing school." Cathy is clearly fascinated by the glamorous Melanie, and excitedly engages her in conversation. She tells Melanie that the people Mitch deals with in his practice as a lawyer in San Francisco are "mostly hoods." Lydia is appalled at her language and corrects her with a pious speech: "In a democracy, Cathy, everyone is entitled to a fair trial. Your brother's practice . . ." But her more realistic daughter cuts her off: "Mom, please, I know all that democracy jazz. They're still hoods." As the story progresses, we will find that increasingly the characters are forced to abandon their illusions.

The screenplay contains an amusing exchange between Melanie and Cathy which does not make it into the film. Melanie is smoking and Cathy begs her for "a little puff," while her mother and brother are in the kitchen cleaning up. Surprisingly, Melanie consents and Cathy takes a puff on her cigarette. "Why, it's just like air, isn't it?" exclaims Cathy. "When I grow up, I'm gonna smoke like a chimney!" It's likely that this exchange was eliminated for the obvious reason that it would encourage smoking in children, and there is no evidence it was ever shot. It serves to reinforce our impression that Melanie is irresponsible. And it is precisely her irresponsibility that Mitch and Lydia are meanwhile discussing in the kitchen. "She's always mentioned in the columns, Mitch," Lydia says while washing up. "She is the one who jumped into that fountain in Rome last summer, isn't she? I know it was supposed to be very warm there, Mitch, but . . . well . . . actually . . . the newspaper said she was naked."

Mitch assures her that he can handle Melanie Daniels and, as the evening draws to a close, he sees the young woman to her car. Cathy has been begging Melanie to stay for her birthday party the following day. It's supposed to be a surprise, but the cat's out of the bag, and Cathy has figured out the whole thing. Mitch also tries to persuade Melanie to attend the party, but she insists that she has to return to San Francisco. Their parting conversation quickly turns into another cross examination, with Mitch playfully interrogating her about the Rome incident, and about her real reason for coming to Bodega Bay. She admits that she doesn't know Annie Hayworth. Amused, Mitch says he would like to see her again, as it might be "fun." But his teasing has gone too far. "That might have been good enough for Rome. But it's not good enough now," she says angrily, and drives off into the night. As he watches her car disappear down the road, Mitch suddenly looks up at the telephone wires and sees hundreds of crows perched on them, their black feathers shimmering in the moonlight. He seems momentarily unnerved by the sight, then returns to the house.

Melanie's remark about Rome is the first real hint of any depth in her; any sense that she may be dissatisfied with her life. Prior to this, she has seemed almost entirely self-satisfied and self-absorbed. In an upcoming scene, we will see her in an even more introspective and self-critical mood. Film critic Andrew Sarris has made some insightful observations about the film's characters:

The theme [of *The Birds*] is complacency, as the director has stated on innumerable occasions. When we first meet each of the major characters, their infinite capacity of self-absorption is emphasized. Tippi Hedren's bored socialite is addicted to elaborately time-consuming practical jokes. Rod Taylor's self-righteous lawyer flaunts his arrogant sensuality, Suzanne Pleshette, his ex-fiancée, wallows in self-pity, and Jessica Tandy, his possessive mother, cringes from her fear of loneliness. With such complex, unsympathetic characters to contend with, the audience begins to identify with the point of view of the birds, actually the inhuman point of view.[5]

There is a great deal of truth in this. And Hitchcock's films frequently feature characters who undergo a crisis and achieve a kind of awakening, shocking them out of their complacency and inertia. This is the theme, for example, of *North by Northwest* (1959). A bored, jaded advertising executive (played by Cary Grant) is accidentally flung into the world of espionage. In order to save his life and that of the first woman he's ever really cared for, he must learn overnight how to be a man. The film also features an element common to many of Hitchcock's films, including *The Birds*: the male protagonist has an unusually close relationship to his mother.

Indeed, Roger Thornhill is set off on his perilous adventures when he hails a bellboy in the Oak Bar of the Plaza Hotel in order to send a telegram to his mother, about whom he is fretting. Just as in *The Birds*, the actress who plays Cary Grant's mother (Jessie Royce Lan-

---

[5] Andrew Sarris, *"You Ain't Heard Nothin' Yet": The American Talking Film History and Memory, 1927–1949* (New York: Oxford University Press, 1998), 297.

dis) seems too young to actually be his mother (and she certainly is: Landis was only *eight* years older than Grant). The classic example of the Hitchcock mother-son relationship, of course, is *Psycho* (1960). And, as many have pointed out, that film also prominently features birds, in the form of Norman Bates' stuffed birds. Of course, the mother on whom he dotes is stuffed as well, though Norman keeps her memory alive (so to speak) by dressing up in her clothes now and then and committing murder. His first victim in the film has the surname Crane.

The "Oedipal" dimension to *The Birds* is explicitly explored in its next scene, when Melanie returns to Annie's house. Annie senses that Melanie's evening has not been all that she'd hoped for and intuits that Lydia is responsible. Offering Melanie a brandy, she refers to Lydia, asking "Did she seem a trifle distant?" Annie now reveals what we already suspected, that she and Mitch had a relationship in the past. Although she doesn't lay the blame squarely with Lydia, it's clear that the older woman sabotaged things. Annie struggled to understand what she had done to displease Lydia, and then realized in time she hadn't done anything at all. "I simply existed. So what was the answer? A jealous woman, right? A clinging, possessive mother? Wrong. With all due respect to Oedipus, I don't think that was the case at all."

This is obviously a highly interesting line. It is an example of "postmodern irony": the screenwriter heads off critics who would inevitably brand the situation "Oedipal" by making the connection himself. But Annie seems too quick to disavow the "Oedipal" label. When Melanie presses her on what's really going on with Lydia, Annie says that she is "Afraid of any woman who'd give Mitch the only thing Lydia can't give him—love." Melanie articulates our own skepticism when she responds, "That adds up to a jealous, possessive woman." But Annie explains: "She's not afraid of losing her son, you see. She's only afraid of being abandoned." In a later scene between Melanie and Lydia, the latter seems to confirm this interpretation of her psychology.

The set for Annie's living room is dressed to suggest that she graduated from a liberal arts college, possibly a girl's school. The walls feature original art, tasteful modern furniture, and an LP of *Tristan und Isolde* sitting atop the stereo cabinet (clearly intended as a joke). Annie no doubt learned about the Oedipus complex in Psych 101. But clearly she didn't major in the subject, as she's got her Freud wrong. What is crucial in the Oedipus complex is *not* the mother's attitude toward the son, but the reverse. Everything Annie has said about Lydia might be true, but the situation could still be Oedipal. Indeed, if Freud is to be believed, Mitch's situation is every little boy's dream, as daddy is finally out of the picture, and he has mommy entirely to himself. He is the "man of the house" now, and an unacknowledged father figure to his much younger sister.

Like Roger Thornhill, however, Mitch isn't actually a man. He's a boy playing at being a man; playing house with his mother and with the affections of women without ever committing in any serious way and starting a life of his own. Poor Annie tells Melanie that their relationship just petered out after a while, as a result of Lydia's attitude. "I can understand his position. He went through a lot with Lydia after his father died. He didn't want to risk going through it all over again." She sees Mitch as noble. Actually, this just makes him seem like a weakling and a momma's boy. And Annie seems a bit pathetic herself, as she reveals that she relocated to Bodega Bay just to be near Mitch—*after* the relationship was over. She too is *stuck*.

In the end, all of the central characters in the film—Melanie, Mitch, Lydia, and Annie—will in one way or another overcome their inertia and grow (though in poor Annie's case it comes just at the end). And they will grow through being placed, with apologies to Freud, in a *primal scene*. The struggle against nature will make a man of Mitch, a mature woman of Melanie, a (healthy) mother of Lydia, and a martyr of Annie. In every case, their eyes are opened—but only as a result of their encounter with something that can be seen but *not* understood.

Blindness is a recurring motif in the film, as we shall see. And let us not forget that the real point of *Oedipus Rex* was the title character's discovery of his own blindness. He imagined that he could see but comes to realize he could not. In the end, he punishes himself for this blindness by gouging out his own eyes. Humanity, in *The Birds*, is about to be taught a similar lesson about its own blindness.

As Melanie and Annie are talking, Mitch calls the house. Annie's entire demeanor softens when she picks up the phone and realizes who it is. But Mitch has called to speak to Melanie. In a Bergmanesque shot, Hitchcock places Annie in the foreground, listening resignedly while Melanie talks to Mitch in the background. He has called to apologize and to try again to persuade her to stay for the birthday party the following day. This time she relents and agrees to attend, saying that of course she doesn't want to disappoint Cathy (yet more disingenuousness). Melanie hangs up, after bidding him good night.

Just as Melanie and Annie are about to retire, there is a loud THUMP at the front door. "Who is it?" Annie inquires, surprised to be disturbed so late. When there is no answer, she opens the door and then speaks (as the script specifies) "to the emptiness outside," saying "Is anyone there?"

"Look!" Melanie cries, pointing downward. There is a dead seagull on the doormat. "Oh, the poor thing," Annie says. "He probably lost his way in the dark."

"But it isn't dark, Annie. There's a full moon," Melanie responds. The two exchange significant looks, and we FADE OUT.

CHAPTER TWO

The next day, Melanie attends Cathy's birthday party, as promised. It is held outdoors at the Brenner home, behind the house. A dozen or more children are present, along with some parents. Annie is also on hand, to help. Colorful balloons have been strung up, and there is a long table covered in cake and other treats. Mitch and Melanie (still wearing her green suit) have been drinking and decide to leave the party briefly while the children play.

They walk up onto one of the dunes behind the house. Mitch is carrying a carafe in which he has mixed martinis, and two glasses. At this point, there is a jarring cut onto what is very obviously an interior studio set recreating the dune, with a painted backdrop of the bay. Technically, this is the low point in a film that already contains quite a few unrealistic shots and special effects. Audiences in 1963 would also have detected the phoniness of this transition to a soundstage, but it was a convention they were willing to accept. Today's audiences are not as forgiving.

The truth is that Hitchcock could easily have avoided this obvious artificiality by simply shooting the entire scene on location. But, as Tippi Hedren has explained on more than one occasion, he wanted to avoid location shooting as much as possible so as to photograph scenes under controlled lighting (especially closeups). This is obviously a reflection of Hitchcock's character: by all accounts, he was an advanced "control freak," something Hedren had to contend with throughout the making of both this film and *Marnie* (1964). For example, Hitchcock had Edith Head design a wardrobe for the actress to wear *off set*, insisted on placing single quotation marks around her nickname 'Tippi' (her given name was Nathalie), and made increasing demands on her time.

The scene on the dunes is also interesting because it was here (and elsewhere) that Hitchcock insisted on certain "improvements" to Evan Hunter's script. Melanie reluctantly partakes of Mitch's martinis, saying that she is concerned about driving home. He frankly admits that he is trying to get her to stay for dinner. "What's so important in San Francisco?" Mitch asks. Much to his amusement, she explains that she needs to go to work. Incredulous, he says "You have a job?" "I have several jobs," she responds proudly. She works for travelers' aid at the airport on Mondays and Wednesdays. On Tuesdays she takes a course in general semantics at Berkeley. On Thursdays she meets with a committee that raises money to put "a little Korean boy" through school. On Fridays, Melanie says, jokingly, she sometimes goes to bird shops. "I'm glad you do," Mitch responds, obviously smitten.

Of course, none of these is a real "job." This information serves to reinforce our impression that Melanie is not just a spoiled little rich girl but also a lost soul. Her project to raise money for a Korean boy rather than, say, a white American boy from the Ozarks, illustrates her detachment from the affairs of ordinary folks and, of course, from her own tribe. And we will soon see tribalism emerge as one of the themes in *The Birds*. Further, the reason Melanie is taking a general semantics course is to acquire a lot of profane words to teach the myna bird she was trying to buy in the film's first scene—an intended gift for her straitlaced and easily-shocked Aunt Tessa. In Evan Hunter's original script, after she reveals this to Mitch "suddenly, a very serious look comes into Melanie's face." She becomes "serious, introspective." Then she says, "That's silly, isn't it? Teaching a bird to shock my aunt. That's just silly and childish." And, after a pause: "Maybe I ought to go join the other children." With that she descends the dune and returns to the party.

However, Hitchcock had doubts about Hunter's script,

feeling that the characters lacked depth. So, he sought the opinion of actor and writer Hume Cronyn (the husband of Jessica Tandy) who had contributed to the screenplays for *Rope* (1948) and *Under Capricorn* (1949). One of the results of this, apparently, was new dialogue inserted into this scene. In the version that was shot, just after Melanie tells Mitch about the myna bird, he says, jokingly, "You need a mother's love, my child." She responds, sharply, "not my mother!" then goes on to tell him how her mother "ditched" their family when she was a little girl. "You know what a mother's love is," she says with a snarl. But the remark only puzzles Mitch.

When he asks her if she has contact with her mother still, Melanie suddenly turns her back to Mitch and says, sobbing slightly and in a childlike voice, "I don't know where she is." This is then followed by the line which closed the scene in the original script, "Maybe I ought to go join the other children." The new dialogue is intended to lay the groundwork for the suggestion, made clear in the very last scene of the film, that Lydia becomes a kind of surrogate mother to Melanie.[1] However, it has always seemed gratuitous to me, and far less interesting than the film's other subplots and themes. This interlude on the dunes is perhaps the least effective scene in the entire film.

When Mitch and Melanie return to the party, the children are playing blind man's bluff (the first of many references to blindness in the film; see my discussion of this in the last chapter). Cathy is blindfolded and Annie is spin-

---

[1] Hunter strongly objected to these changes to his script, and years later said he had no idea who had written them. In fact, the new dialogue was written by an old friend of Hitchcock's, V. S. Pritchett, a fiction writer who was also book review editor for *The New Statesman*. See Moral, *The Making of Hitchcock's* The Birds, 148.

ning her around, but Annie's eyes are on Mitch and Melanie the entire time. Lydia watches the couple too, with an
expression of great apprehension. Just as Cathy begins to
try to catch the other children, a gull swoops down. "Look!
Look!" cries a little boy. The gull grazes Cathy but she
thinks it is one of the other children. "No touching al-
lowed!" she cries, annoyed. Now gull after gull swoops in,
divebombing the party goers and bursting the balloons.

The gulls ignore the table full of food and seem to deliberately attack the children, who begin screaming in terror and running in all directions. Melanie uses her jacket
to chase off one gull, which has a child pinned to the
grass, pecking at his back. Mitch comes to the aid of another, who is being pursued up the dunes by an angry gull
that seems determined to cause her harm. These shots
were accomplished by actually tying the gulls to the unfortunate child actors! It is one of the more effective attack scenes in the film largely because it seems to have
been accomplished primarily with live birds, and the use
of special photographic effects is minimal.

The adults finally manage to herd the panicked children into the house, and the seagulls disperse just as suddenly as they arrived. Everyone stands just inside the
doors to the veranda, staring up at the sky and trying to
make sense of what has happened. It is at this point in the
film that the characters recognize that a pattern is form-
ing. First there was the gull that struck Melanie, then the
gull that collided with Annie's front door (something
Mitch has not heard about until this moment), and now
the attack on the children's party.

That all the attacks so far involve seagulls seems to be a
deliberate red herring. Our first reaction will be to assume
that something is wrong with the gulls—that these
strange anomalies are confined to them. Our minds look
for the common elements in phenomena we wish to explain. Until we have found the common element, we are

in a state of anxious suspension. When we think we have found some sort of commonality, we feel a sense of relief, for at least (so we suppose) the troubling phenomenon is delimited; it affects this much, and not that. But, in this case, we get a sinking feeling when we remember the chickens; their behavior has been strange as well. As we will see, *all* attempts to explain the bird attacks in this film ultimately fail.

Melanie is decidedly spooked, and it is now easy for Mitch to persuade her to stay for dinner, which takes place in the following scene. Mitch has sliced the leftover roast beef from the previous night, and the foursome (Mitch, Lydia, Cathy, and Melanie) serve themselves, sitting and eating casually in the living room. The adults discuss the best way for Melanie to get back to San Francisco. Lydia is obviously very intent on getting Melanie out of Bodega Bay and shoots Cathy a sharp glance when the little girl, who clearly likes Melanie, suggests that she use their spare bedroom and stay the night. The lovebirds are making a racket in their cage, and just as Cathy notes this fact, Hitchcock's camera focusses on Hedren's face as she looks down and toward the hearth. The actress looks exquisitely beautiful in this shot, which is ever-so-slightly in soft focus. We then see her point of view: a small, brown sparrow suddenly appears out of nowhere, sitting on the hearth. "Mitch," Melanie calls out softly—just as a great torrent of sparrows comes rushing down the chimney and fills the room.

It is an indescribably eerie moment, which always gives me a shiver. There is nothing at all "supernatural" in *The Birds*; no hint that anything like witchery is at work. Yet Hitchcock succeeds from here on out in conveying a very strong sense of the *uncanny*. This is the film's real power.

Old English *cann* means "knowledge," from *cunnan* meaning "to know, to be familiar with" and also "to know how to." (Compare German *kennen* and *können*.) The "canny" is what is known or familiar, and what we have a handle on. (A "canny" person is a "knowing" person whose knowing makes them particularly capable: they know *how to*.) The uncanny is thus not just the unknown or unfamiliar, but something that resists our efforts to get a handle on it, to manipulate it or make it intelligible. The uncanny is thus disconcerting and unsettling. It challenges our power and threatens to overturn our sense that we "have a handle on things" or have things under our control.

We can arrive at a more precise sense of the uncanny by examining its German equivalent: *unheimlich* (adj.; *the* uncanny is *das Unheimliche*). The *heim* in the adjective *heimlich* is cognate with English "home," and so this word really *ought* to mean "familiar" (i.e., "homey"). Yet what *heimlich* actually means in German is "secret" (compare the noun *Geheimnis*, "secret"). This makes *unheimlich* a very strange word, since the *un-* (same as English un-; "not," as in "unhappy") would seem to negate "secret," making the *unheimlich* that which is *no longer secret*, or that which has been revealed. The standard way that linguists deal with this problem is to say that the *heimlich* in *unheimlich* is not the usual *heimlich*; that here it really does mean "familiar" ("homey"), rather than "secret."

In his essay on the uncanny, Freud suggests that matters may be more complicated than this:

> [A]mong the various shades of meaning that are recorded for the word *heimlich* there is one in which it merges with its formal antonym, *unheimlich*, so that what is called *heimlich* becomes *unheimlich*. . . . This reminds us that this word *heimlich* is not unambiguous, but belongs to two sets of ideas, which are not mutually contradictory, but are very different from each other—the one relating to what is familiar and comfortable, the other to what is concealed and kept hidden. *Unheimlich* is the antonym

of *heimlich* only in the latter's first sense, not in its second.[2]

The nature of the uncanny/*Das Unheimliche* may be discovered through understanding this dual sense of being *both*, as it were, "the un-secret" and the "un-homey."[3] *Das Unheimliche* does not mean "the un-secret" in the sense of something that had been hidden and unknown but is now revealed and fully known. Instead, what it means is something hidden that now shows itself but *nonetheless remains hidden*. In other words, to be in the presence of the uncanny is to be confronted with a phenomenon that remains intransigently unintelligible. Something *does* emerge out of hiddenness here, but this something is an enigma. Or, to put it even more simply, in the encounter with the uncanny, a mystery is revealed (while remaining a mystery). (It helps to know, in addition, that in German *Geheimnis* can mean "secret" *or* "mystery.") For this reason, the uncanny is at the same time the un-homey, the fundamentally unfamiliar.

The encounter with the uncanny is a complete and total shock to human consciousness. It occasions a feeling of dread, and the realization that perhaps everything we have thought is *wrong*. It chastens us, as we are brought face to face with our arrogance in thinking we knew, when we did not. We will see that, ultimately, the principal theme of *The Birds* has to do with this encounter with the uncanny.

To return to our story, in a moment the living room fills with what looks like hundreds of small birds. The women panic, but Mitch springs into action. He opens a window and begins trying to fan the birds out of the room

---

[2] Sigmund Freud, "The Uncanny," trans. David McLintok, *The Uncanny* (London: Penguin, 2003), 132.

[3] However, my conclusions here are not those of Freud.

with a towel, then he upends a table and places it against the fireplace. In order to shoot this scene (and others) the entire set was surrounded by polyethylene walls and "bird wranglers" were on hand to deal with the animals.[4] The trouble was that many of the birds failed to exhibit the frenetic activity the director was looking for, and some simply perched on the furniture. Plus, it was necessary to limit the number of birds on set, for the safety of the actors. "Cover your faces! Cover your eyes!" Mitch orders the women, with good reason (it is also a portent of things to come, as we shall see).

The result was that the scene was insufficiently dramatic. Hitchcock solved this problem by engaging the services of Disney's veteran visual effects man Ub Iwerks (among other things, the designer of Oswald the Lucky Rabbit and Mickey Mouse). Iwerks took footage of birds flying inside a glass booth and, using an optical printer, superimposed that footage onto the film taken on set. For this, and his work on other scenes in *The Birds*, Iwerks was nominated for an Academy Award.

In this scene, at least, the result of Iwerk's labors is pretty good but not perfect. It is clear to the audience that some trick is involved, as there appears to be a surface level of bird images that is "flat" and with which the actors do not interact. At the same time, however, we can clearly see that there is *depth* to the composite image as a whole: some birds are clearly on set and flying through the room. This causes us to question our initial judgment and to suspend disbelief and become caught up in the drama of the scene. After the characters escape through a side door

---

[4] Despite the crew's best efforts, some of the birds escaped and roosted in the soundstage. They stayed well past the conclusion of filming on *The Birds*, chirping in the rafters and bedeviling the sound men on later films. See Moral, *The Making of Hitchcock's* The Birds, 129.

into another part of the house, the final shot of this sequence shows the room filled with hundreds of actual birds. This causes us, subconsciously, to question whether we were right in thinking there was anything "fake" here at all—at least on an initial viewing. The entire technique is very clever, and, on the whole, it's one of the most effective scenes in the film.

The sheriff is summoned, but his uselessness is quickly made apparent when he picks up a dead bird from the living room floor and says, "That's a sparrow, all right." The Brenners want him to "do something." But, in fairness, what can he do? "Those birds *attacked*," says Lydia forcefully, referring to the behavior of the gulls at Cathy's party. "Now, Lydia, 'attack' is a pretty strong word, don't you think?" the sheriff responds. "I mean, birds just don't go around attacking people without no reason, you know what I mean? The kids just probably scared them, that's all." But Lydia is insistent: "These birds attacked!" As we shall see, of all the characters in the film, Lydia may be the one who sees most clearly that they are now in an "us vs. them" situation. The sheriff departs, and much to Lydia's consternation, Mitch suggests that Melanie stay the night. She responds, "I think I should, don't you?" Despite her intentions, she has become emotionally involved with this family, and chooses now to share their fate.

The next morning, we see Melanie rise from bed in her unpretentious night dress. We also hear the voices of Mitch and Lydia. The latter is saying that she intends to visit Dan Fawcett's farm after dropping Cathy at school, presumably to ask him about the behavior of his chickens. In the finished film, it is at this point that we dissolve to Lydia arriving at Fawcett's place. In the screenplay, however, there is a scene involving Mitch and Melanie that takes place after Melanie comes downstairs. We know (based on production photos) that this scene was actually shot, but it was omitted from the final cut, and the footage appears lost. It is quite an interesting scene, in fact, and, as a friend of mine put it, "very reactionary."

In the omitted scene, Melanie comes downstairs in her night dress, helps herself to coffee, then steps outside. It's a beautiful day, and her eyes scan the horizon. "There isn't a bird anywhere in sight," Evan Hunter's screenplay specifies. "The day is still and clear, but somehow ominous in its silence." She sees Mitch, across the property, busying himself with a rake. He sees her as well and starts towards her. She watches him approach, "her eyes glowing." But she is disappointed when, instead of joining her, he enters the house by another door. Mitch quickly re-emerges, however. He has changed his shirt, and walks towards her, buttoning it. (The intention here was probably to give the audience a glimpse of Rod Taylor's skin; handsome, virile actors were constantly changing their shirts in films of the time.)

"It's hard to believe anything at all happened yesterday, isn't it? It's so beautiful and still now," Melanie says. But then she tells him, mischievously, that she thinks she's "got it all figured out." Mitch asks her to explain. "It's an uprising," she says, her tongue in cheek. "It all started a few months ago with a peasant sparrow up in the hills, a malcontent. He went around telling all the other sparrows that human beings weren't fit to rule this planet, preaching wherever anyone would listen . . ."

"Growing a beard!" Mitch interjects. Today's audiences might not understand such a reference, but in the fifties and sixties having a beard was usually taken as evidence of radicalism. Melanie is delighted by this. "Yes, of course, he had to have a beard! 'Birds of the world, unite!' he kept saying, over and over . . . Eventually, even the more serious-minded birds began to listen. 'Why should humans rule?'. . . Why should we submit ourselves to their domination? . . . And all the while, that sparrow was getting in his little messages. Birds of the world, unite! . . . You have nothing to lose but your feathers."

Hunter tells us, "They both burst out laughing, then fall into silence, then laugh again and finally are silent. The garden is deathly still." Silence is one of the film's most notable features, and it is used repeatedly to create suspense, and to suggest the presence of the uncanny. One might think that this was Hitchcock's contribution, yet the screenplay references "silence" or things being "silent" fifty-nine times (the word "still" is used in the sense of "silent" an additional ten times).

Mitch suddenly tries to be serious, reassuring Melanie that the birds are probably just hungry (this is an explanation that is repeated throughout the film, despite being refuted again and again). "With my little sparrow leading the team," she says. They laugh again, but now it feels forced. "Like children who have told themselves a too realistic horror story, they are becoming a little frightened." "It's so damn quiet out there," Mitch says. "It makes you feel as if they're . . . they're waiting or . . . resting . . . or . . ." Melanie responds, struggling to articulate an intuition. Seeing that she's frightened, Mitch tries humor again. "No, they're having a meeting, Melanie. Your sparrow is standing on a soap box and . . ."

He cuts himself off when he sees that the expression on her face is deadly serious. "His voice trails. His face becomes serious, too. Again, the garden is silent." There is a close shot of Melanie, "her face set and grim, her eyes serious, her words coming slowly and with the chill of horror on them." "They were angry," she says. "They came out of the chimney in fury. I had the feeling they wanted each and every one of us dead." This is an observation that will be repeated later on, in a memorable scene set in the Tides Restaurant.

Mitch takes Melanie in his arms, trying to comfort her. "I'm frightened," she says. "I'm frightened and confused and I . . . I think I want to go back to San Francisco where there are buildings and . . . and concrete and . . . everything I know." This is, of course, the natural human response to an encounter with the uncanny. One wants to retreat into the familiar. In this case, it seems that nature has turned on them, revealing itself in a new and inexplicable way. So naturally Melanie wants to return to the world of "buildings and concrete," the human-contrived world which we think we can control. She looks up at him and says, "Oh damn it, why did you have to walk into that shop?" It is an annoying line, and it results in the inevitable kiss. Here, the scene shifts to Lydia's arrival at the Fawcett farm.

So why was this scene cut? It surely cannot have been to avoid offending communists. (Hitchcock's films are generally so anti-communist they've been labelled "reactionary" by left-wing critics.) Until its final moments, the scene is something of a return to the lighthearted tone of the beginning of the film, so perhaps it was cut because Hitchcock wanted to maintain the atmosphere of impending doom established in the preceding scenes. Perhaps he thought it slowed the pace of the film. Perhaps he was unhappy with the performances.

All these suggestions could be true, but I believe there is a further, very important reason why the scene was cut. Hitchcock wanted to remove from the film any explanations of *why* the birds are attacking, other than the ones that were most banal and obviously wrong (e.g., "they're hungry"). Melanie's Marxist parable is obviously intended in jest. But Hitchcock may have been concerned that it would nonetheless encourage the idea that the birds have turned on humanity as some kind of revenge for man's mistreatment of them, or of nature in general. This was the explicit theme of the godawful 1994 made-for-cable sequel *The Birds II: Land's End*, directed by the prolific Alan Smithee. Hedren had a small cameo in that film but regretted it. At the time, she justified her appearance by saying "it has helped me to feed my lions and tigers." But years later she said, "It's absolutely horrible. It embarrasses me horribly." As we will see, Hitchcock deleted other material from Hunter's screenplay in which characters offer explanations for why the birds are attacking. Ultimately, he wanted the entire thing to be unexplained, and inexplicable.

We now transition to one of the most famous scenes in the film. Lydia arrives in her pickup truck at Dan Fawcett's place. One of the farm hands says he hasn't seen the old man so far that morning, but that he must be inside the house. Lydia knocks at the front door. When there is no answer, she hesitantly lets herself into the kitchen and calls out "Dan, are you home?" "The house is still and silent," Hunter's script tells us. And there is still no response from Mr. Fawcett. Lydia moves further into the kitchen, and then suddenly something catches her eye. A number of teacups hanging from hooks under the credenza have all been broken. The camera moves in on Lydia, taking in her reaction. We can tell from the look on her face that she knows, immediately, what has happened. It is a chilling moment.

Against her better judgment, Lydia now enters the corridor to the bedrooms. The suspense of this moment is impossible to describe, nor is it possible (for this writer, at least) to explain how Hitchcock manages to create such suspense, and such ominousness, from a simple shot of a woman moving hesitantly down a dimly lit corridor. Silence is, again, an important element. Lydia finds the door to Fawcett's bedroom ajar. She peers into the room and sees that it is a complete shambles. In staging this scene, Hitchcock followed Hunter's description of the setting very precisely, so it is worth quoting it here:

A standing floor lamp, the shade dangling, but the light still burning; a picture hanging askew on the wall, its glass shattered; the window to the left of the picture, every pane of glass shattered; a dresser with two stuffed birds on its top; both birds have been badly damaged, the stuffing ripped out of them, the head of one hanging at a crooked near decapitated angle; the window to the left of the dresser, all the panes shattered.

I have always found the inclusion of stuffed birds here very odd (as if there weren't enough live birds in the movie!). Hitchcock also adds a dead gull, smashed against the outside of the broken window. The camera follows Lydia's point of view as she scans the room. Her eyes turn to the floor, behind the door. We see a pair of bare feet and the ends of tattered and bloody pajama bottoms. Lydia's eyes widen in horror—but she must, she simply *must* continue looking. She peers behind the door to see that the legs belong to the unfortunate Dan Fawcett, lying dead on the floor, face covered in blood, with two black holes where his eyes once were. Fawcett's face is revealed in a triple jump cut, each shot nearer to the man's awful face, ending in a tight closeup. Hitchcock pulls us in, and we are *forced* to look, just as Lydia is.[5]

The shots of Fawcett's face are genuinely horrifying, and it is possibly the grisliest moment in any Hitchcock film (more graphic than anything in *Psycho*). This scene is guaranteed to shut up jaded, modern viewers who may have jeered the lack of realism in earlier parts of the film. Audiences generally assume that the effect was accomplished with very good make up. What is fascinating is that it was actually accomplished with a matte painting.

---

[5] Hitchcock also said that he used the jump cut in case there was any problem with the censors. If they objected to the gore, they could snip out the two closer shots. See Moral, *The Making of Hitchcock's* The Birds, 132.

For the uninitiated, a matte painting is a cinematic special effect in which part of a setting is painted onto a sheet of glass. The camera photographs the setting through the glass, creating the illusion that what is in the painting is actually physically present. As noted in the last chapter, a matte painting of Hitchcock's fictitious version of Bodega Bay is used in the scene when Melanie cuts across the water in the motorboat. When Hitchcock showed that particular scene to one of his assistants, she remarked "It looks just like a painting." He was concerned, thinking that she could see through the artifice. In fact, she thought the footage was of the actual town and meant that she thought the shot was so beautiful it *could* be a painting!

The art of creating such beautiful but realistic matte paintings is now mostly "lost," since it has been superseded by CGI (which I honestly find far less impressive than matte paintings, and no more "realistic"). The acknowledged master of the art was the late, great Albert Whitlock, who produced the paintings for *The Birds*. Whitlock had first worked with Hitchcock in England in the 1930s. In this scene, he painted two very black dots on a sheet of glass, and the actor playing Dan Fawcett (face already daubed with fake blood by the makeup man) was photographed through it. The result is that we feel we are staring into two black abysses. The effect is deeply unsettling.

What happens next is, arguably, just as dramatic. Utterly traumatized, Lydia drops her handbag and half staggers, half runs down the corridor and out of the house. The screenplay specifies that she utters a "terrified scream" and that she continues screaming, "as if she is unable to stop it." When it came time to film the scene, however, Hitchcock decided to have Jessica Tandy do the *exact opposite* of this. Once again, silence dominates. Instead of screaming, Lydia has what psychologists call a "hysterical reaction": she is temporarily unable to scream or to speak. She careens down the corridor, mouth agape, struggling to scream, then exits the house. Camera stationed at the front gate, Hitchcock shoots Tandy at a low angle as she rushes out of the house, stopping for a moment next to the confused farm hand, head tilted toward the sky, gagging slightly, still struggling to scream. It is an Oscar-worthy performance from Tandy, who is excellent in the entire film.[6]

Lydia climbs into her truck and drives at breakneck speed back to her own house. (Hitchcock made sure the road from the Fawcett farm was covered in fuller's earth so that the truck would kick up lots of dust.) When she arrives back at the house, Mitch and Melanie are together in the driveway. She clambers out of the car and Mitch can immediately see that something is very wrong. But seeing her son together with Melanie is more than Lydia can take right now. Sobbing, she pushes them apart and rushes into the house.

---

[6] Hitchcock remarked at the time, "I had [Jessica Tandy] run up from a distance and then bring her up to a big head when she's inarticulate. The sound of her running feet should match the size of the image and, when she gets into the truck, the sound of anguish, which I hope to stylise, will be the whine of the engine on the truck. In other words we are really experimenting here by taking real sounds and then stylising them, so we could abstract a little more drama out of ordinary sounds than we would normally do." See Moral, *The Making of Hitchcock's* The Birds, 117.

CHAPTER THREE

The police are called, and Mitch is asked to meet the sheriff at the Fawcett farm. Detectives from Santa Rosa are going to join them there. Presumably, Mitch is expected to repeat his mother's account of finding the corpse of Dan Fawcett, its eyes pecked out by homicidal birds. In any case, Lydia is in no condition to tell the story herself. Mitch and Melanie talk quietly in the kitchen while the latter makes a pot of tea to take to Lydia.

They embrace. "Do be careful, please," Melanie says, and then they kiss. This sudden display of affection between the pair is somewhat jarring to the viewer, but only because the earlier scene in which they kiss was cut from the film. In the absence of that scene, the casualness with which they express affection here is rather touching. It feels as if it is simply a natural and spontaneous result of the way that events have flung the two together. The teasing and sparring have now vanished from their relationship. They seem somehow more mature and interact as if they have been a couple for some time. In fact, Mitch and Melanie have only known each other for three days (in case the reader has forgotten, they met on Friday and now it is Monday). This is the effect that adversity can have on men and women.

Mitch departs and Melanie carries the tea to Lydia's room, which is on the ground floor. Hunter's screenplay describes Lydia's room as "cluttered with the mementos of a life no longer valid. There are photographs of her dead husband, souvenirs of trips taken together, bric-a-brac of Mitch's childhood. Under it all, there is a distinct femininity." Lydia is lying in bed. This time, she seems rather glad to see Melanie (who calls her "Mrs. Brenner"). Clearly still traumatized by what she had seen at the Fawcett farm,

Lydia's conversation is somewhat scattered. Uppermost in her mind is Cathy's safety. "I keep seeing Dan's face," she says. "They have such big windows at the school. All the windows were broken in Dan's bedroom. All the windows."

Melanie reassures her that Cathy will be okay, but Lydia is not convinced, and neither are we. "I'm not usually this way, you know. I don't fuss and fret over my children," she says. Given how cold she has been so far in this film, we wish she would fuss and fret a bit more. Lydia realizes that she lacks something and begins to reminisce about her husband. "When Frank died . . . You see, he knew the children, he really knew them. He had the knack of being able to enter into their world, of becoming a part of them. That's a rare talent . . . I wish I could be that way." It now becomes clear to us that Cathy has been so keen on Melanie staying with them because she is seeking something from the younger woman that she cannot get from her mother.

Hunter writes, "There is another silence. A curious thing is happening in this room. Lydia, for perhaps the first time since her husband's death, is discussing it with another person. Curiously, the person is Melanie." Indeed, Lydia now seems to be warming to her. Melanie offers to leave and let her rest. "No. No . . . don't go yet," Lydia says. "I feel as if I don't understand you. And I want so much to understand."

Melanie asks her why. "Because my son seems to be very fond of you," Lydia answers. "And I'm not quite sure how I feel about it. I don't even know if I like you or not." This is said completely without malice. It is a moment of simple and plain honesty. Melanie insists that it doesn't really matter whether Lydia likes her or not, though we know that actually it matters very much matters to Melanie. She has already heard from Annie what Lydia can do to Mitch's relationships.

"Mitch has always done exactly what he wanted to do," Lydia says with resignation. Then, in the screenplay but not in the finished film, she adds "That's the mark of a man." Of course, she misunderstands her son. He has always done what *she* has wanted him to do, and thus does *not* bear the mark of a man. Suggesting that she is dimly aware of her manipulation of him (and of her own motivations), Lydia becomes emotional at this point and says, "But you see, I . . . I wouldn't want to be left alone. I don't think I could bear to be left alone. Oh, forgive me." She begins sobbing and Melanie, who is obviously moved, tries to comfort her.

Lydia has confirmed Annie's analysis of her psychology: she interferes in Mitch's relationships out of a fear of being abandoned. Nevertheless, as I noted in chapter one, Annie is blind to Mitch's own complicity in Lydia's interference, and to Mitch's weakness. Each of the major characters in the film has been abandoned. Abandonment is a major theme of *The Birds*.

The characters have been abandoned in relationships, and in a "metaphysical" way (as I shall argue later).

Lydia is uncharacteristically emotional and volatile in this scene. Much has been made of how the character of Melanie is "broken down" by the film's end (often coupled with sinister speculations about Hitchcock's motives toward Tippi Hedren). But more than one character is "broken down" in this film, and Lydia is the first of the women. Her trauma at the Fawcett farm (quite literally a trauma, complete with hysterical reaction) has precipitated a crisis, and now the catharsis has come. Her veneer of cool control has been shattered, and she has been forced to confront herself and her shortcomings.

Lydia's thoughts swing back to Cathy. "Do you think she's safe at the school?" she asks again, seeking more reassurance. At this point, Melanie offers to go and fetch Cathy, just to be safe. Lydia is effusive in her thanks. Just as Melanie is about to leave the room, Lydia calls to her. "Melanie?" she says, warmly. "Thanks for the tea."

The setting now shifts to the exterior of the Bodega Bay school, in the middle of the afternoon. We are now in store for what is arguably the film's most iconic scene. As Melanie parks her Aston Martin in front of the building, we hear the children singing "Risseldy Rosseldy," an American version of the Scottish folk song "Wee Cooper O'Fife." Hunter's screenplay specifies this, and even includes every line of the original song:

> I married my wife
> In the month of June,
> Risseldy, rosseldy,
> Mow, mow, mow,
> I carried her off
> In a silver spoon,
> Risseldy, Rosseldy,
> Hey bambassity,
> Nickety, nackety,
> Retrical quality,
> Willowby, wallowby,
> Mow, mow, mow.
>
> She combed her hair
> But once a year,
> Risseldy, rosseldy,
> Mow, mow, mow,
> With every rake
> She shed a tear,
> Risseldy, Rosseldy,
> Hey bambassity,
> Nickety, nackety,
> Retrical quality,
> Willowby, wallowby,
> Mow, mow, mow . . .

And so on. It was realized later that the song was not long enough to cover the entire scene in the film. So, at Hitchcock's request, Hunter wrote two more stanzas. In order to use Hunter's new lyrics, however, the writer had to join the American Society of Composers and Publishers. Hunter remarked years later, "I still get royalties from ASCAP on *The Birds* for the lyrics I wrote for that scene."[1]

The song is about sixty percent nonsense words, but it is clear that its subject is a woman who is spoiled and thoroughly undomestic. In other words, she has no idea how to be a woman, in the traditional sense. The story is told from the perspective of her husband. When they were married, he "carried her off in a silver spoon," indicating that she is treated with exceptional consideration, probably because that is what she is accustomed to. ("Back in your gilded cage, Melanie Daniels," says Mitch in the film's first scene, as he replaces a loose canary in its cage.)

Intolerably lazy, "She combed her hair but once a year." And she could certainly not be expected to work on her husband's farm (remember that Mitch and his family are technically farmers): "With every rake she shed a tear," and "She swept the floor but once a year," given that she "swore her broom was much too dear." Further, she was hopeless at whatever she attempted: "She churned her butter in dad's old boot. And for a dasher used her foot. The butter came out a grizzly gray." To make matters worse, "The cheese took legs and ran away."[2]

The Birds prominently features dysfunctional, modern relationships between men and women, and parents and children. Things are topsy-turvy in the Mitch-Melanie relationship. He is the pursued, and she the pursuer. (Just

---

[1] See Moral, *The Making of Hitchcock's* The Birds, 49.

[2] The complete lyrics to the song can be found in Christopher Laws, "*The Birds* (1963): 'Risseldy Rosseldy,'" *Culturedarm*, no date.

as, before Melanie, Annie had pursued Mitch to Bodega Bay.) Mitch is a grown man, whose manner and appearance are quite masculine, yet he is caught in an infantile relationship with his mother. Mitch calls her "dear" and "darling," terms of endearment we usually associate with married couples. Because of this relationship, Mitch is unable to make a real connection with another woman. Lydia is the anti-mother, who places her own needs above those of her son and sabotages his relationships. The father, needless to say, is absent—save for his portrait, which gazes out at the family from the living room wall. Cathy is a smart aleck who contradicts her mother, and seems, as I mentioned earlier, to be seeking something from Melanie that Lydia cannot provide. Melanie (as we will see a little later) calls her father "daddy." Development has been arrested. Roles have been reversed or betrayed.

Nature cannot be denied for long, however. Either what had been unnatural comes to align itself with nature, or nature finds some way to strike back. This is at least part of what the bird attacks signify in this film (though I shall argue later that a deeper level of interpretation is possible). As others have pointed out, "the birds" can be understood as referring to the women in the film ("bird" is British slang for woman). It is, of course, chiefly women who maintain the closest tie to nature, since they feel the call of the natural, sub-rational "self" more strongly than men do.

In *The Birds* we find an assortment of women who seem out of alignment with that natural self. But whenever this occurs it is never women themselves who are to blame, it is their men. It is through her relationship to a man that a woman truly finds this alignment. By contrast, men become men primarily through direct confrontation with nature, or other men. One of the results of Hunter and Hitchcock's story is that these topsy-turvy relationships become realigned with what is natural. Mitch becomes a man, Melanie a woman, and Lydia a loving and accepting mother. But more about that later.

Melanie enters the building to find Annie leading the children in the song. She indicates wordlessly that she needs to speak with Annie, and the latter signals that they will be finished in a minute. Melanie exits and, trying to kill time, she sits down on a bench next to the fence surrounding the schoolyard. The children continue to sing. Directly behind Melanie there is a jungle gym on the playground. Sometimes called "monkey bars," this is an American invention which has been a fixture of parks and playgrounds in the US since the 1920s (though in today's safety-obsessed culture, some have now been removed).

Melanie is clearly nervous and impatient for the children to finish their song. Behind her, we see a single crow land on the jungle gym. Melanie now takes a cigarette out of its pack and fishes in her handbag for a lighter. By the time she has found it and lighted the cigarette, three more crows have perched on the jungle gym. Then another— and another, and another. Hitchcock cuts back and forth between Melanie and the jungle gym. But then he focusses entirely on Melanie, showing her in close up smoking her cigarette, in a shot that lasts slightly less than twenty-eight seconds—but feels at least twice as long. This is audience manipulation at its most diabolical. We long to see whether more crows have gathered on the jungle gym, but Hitchcock refuses us this. It was his deliberate intention to hold the closeup of Hedren "until the audience can't stand it anymore."

The suspense is unbearable. Somehow, the children's monotonous song only heightens it, and intensifies our horror (perhaps because of the contrast between the innocence of the children's voices, and the malevolence of the gathering crows). Something in the air catches Melanie's eye. Finally, Hitchcock cuts away from Melanie to show her point of view: a single crow flying high above. Electrified, she follows it as it comes to land on the jungle gym—joining what is now a huge flock of crows. A murder of crows, in fact. Melanie rises from the bench, recoiling in horror from the sight of the birds (here, the closeup of Hedren is obviously a shot re-created in the studio, and not taken on location). In scenes such as this, by the way, some of the birds were stuffed props and others were mere cardboard cutouts. Real birds, twitching and fluttering, were placed strategically next to these, usually tied to whatever they were perching on. The power of suggestion causes the audience to assume that all of the birds are real.

Hurrying, but moving as silently as she can, Melanie enters the school—just as Annie is opening the side door leading onto the playground! Melanie pleads with her to close it, and points out the window and toward the jungle gym. "Look!" The schoolhouse is extremely vulnerable to attack, since, as Lydia mentioned, it has so many large windows. Annie and Melanie conclude that the only course of action is to get the children out of the building and down the road. Amid the youngsters' rather comical protests, Annie tells them that they are going to leave the school as quietly as possible and head toward the town. When she gives the signal, they will begin to run. (It is somewhat sad to see these scenes of a well-dressed, well-behaved, and all-white class: a visual record of an America that no longer exists.)

At this point, a less imaginative director would show us the children tip toeing out of the school. Hitchcock finds a brilliant alternative to this. He does not show us the children at all—not yet, anyway. Instead, his camera focusses on the crows massed on the jungle gym. For fifteen long seconds he holds this shot. Then we hear the sound of the children's feet. Annie has given the signal, and they are running. All at once, the crows take flight. They have been waiting for just this moment. This is the first time in the film that we seem to experience the action from the perspective of the birds.

We then see the children running down the hill, away from the school and toward town. What follows is one of the most technically complicated sequences in the entire film. Footage was taken of the screaming children running away from the school and running down the road toward the main part of town (actually, two completely different locations, in different towns). The children, along with Hedren and Pleshette, were then photographed on a soundstage running on a treadmill against a process shot.

These shots feature the performers interacting sometimes with real birds, sometimes obvious fakes. However, the shots are intercut rapidly so that we cannot focus on anything for too long. This reduces the impression of fakery, and very successfully causes us to suspend disbelief and to become emotionally involved in the plight of the characters.

At several points, certain children appear to be in real jeopardy. One little boy is pursued by a crow around a telephone pole. A little girl pitches forward onto the ground, the glasses flying from her face. Hitchcock shows us the thick, shattered eyeglasses in a closeup (another reference to "blindness").

The majority of the birds shown in the sequence were the result of optical effects. Once all the footage had been shot, it was delivered to Disney Studios' master technician Ub Iwerks, who used a "yellow screen" sodium vapor process to layer images of birds onto the footage. This process, superior to "blue screen," was used very successfully by Disney in a number of films, notably *Mary Poppins* (1964). The result, predictably, looks a bit like a Disney cartoon. This is especially the case at the beginning of the sequence, when we see the birds fly over the schoolhouse and toward the children. It is obviously fake—but it is a good fake. In addition to Iwerks, Bill Abbott of 20th Century Fox worked on the visual effects for the crows. With two teams each working eleven hours a day, it still took six weeks to finish work on the scene.

Cathy comes to the aid of the little girl with the broken glasses (whose name in the screenplay is Michele). Together with Melanie, they seek refuge in an unlocked car. Melanie's intention is to get the car going and get out of there, but the keys are missing. Crows descend on the car and, reduced to desperation, Melanie begins blowing the horn. In another moment, however, the crows disperse, and all is quiet once more.

The setting now changes to the interior of the Tides Restaurant, which, in the film's revision of the real Bodega Bay, is just down the hill from the school. Melanie is standing at the bar talking on the phone to her father who, the reader will recall, is a wealthy newspaper owner in San Francisco. We will learn later that Cathy has been left in the care of Annie Hayworth.

This is one of the most important scenes in the film, rich with indications of its deeper meaning. It is also replete with good dialogue, interesting new characters, and tension. Here, Hitchcock employs "crosstalk," a dramatic technique in which characters talk over each other, which is seldom seen in his films. This helps to create an atmosphere of mounting hysteria, with things seeming to be spinning rapidly out of control.

It is lunchtime, and the restaurant is busy. Watching over the proceedings is the Tides's proprietor, the middle-aged Deke Carter. Flitting busily about the dining room is a dark-haired waitress, who is identified in the script (but not in the film) as Deke's wife, Helen. A "drunk," who is called Jason in the script (but not the film), sits at the bar sipping a beer. Just to make sure we know the man is drunk, the actor (Karl Swenson) speaks with an Irish accent. A gruff fisherman, Sebastian Sholes, sits at a booth hurriedly consuming his lunch. At another booth is a mother with two children, a boy and a girl.

"Daddy, there were hundreds of them," Melanie says into the phone. "No, I'm not hysterical, I'm trying to tell you this as calmly as I know how." Just then, the door opens and in walks Mrs. Bundy. Though she appears only in this one scene, Mrs. Bundy is one of the most significant and memorable characters in the entire film. The script describes her as "sixtyish, wearing walking shoes and a tweed suit, a very masculine-looking woman with short clipped white hair." Actress Ethel Griffies is perfectly cast in the role and is dressed exactly as described.

Griffies, born in Sheffield, England, had made her first stage appearance at the age of three, and at the time of her death in 1975, aged 97, was Britain's oldest working actress. A spry 84 at the time The Birds was shot, she is much older than the Mrs. Bundy described by Hunter, but exceptionally sharp. The actress made a considerable impression upon the inexperienced Tippi Hedren.

Mrs. Bundy has arrived to purchase a pack of cigarettes from the restaurant's machine. When she realizes that Melanie is speaking about birds, she begins to listen in on her conversation. "No, the birds didn't attack until the children were outside the school. Crows, I think. I don't know, Daddy. Is there a difference between crows and blackbirds?" At this point, Mrs. Bundy turns to her and, with great superiority, proclaims "There is very definitely a difference, Miss." Griffies speaks with her own English accent. This, plus the drunken Irishman (from whom we will hear in a moment) plus the variety of American accents in the room, feels strange. (I have already mentioned in chapter one how the proprietor of the general store seems to speak with a Maine accent.) We get the impression that we are dealing not so much with the townsfolk of Bodega Bay as with a cross section of humanity. As I will argue in chapter four, it is humanity itself that is addressed in this scene.

Mrs. Bundy is, as Hunter specifies, quite masculine, and this is accentuated when she begins brandishing a lit cigarette. We get the feeling that she might be the town lesbian. Ironically, she will now lecture us on nature, for Mrs. Bundy is an amateur ornithologist. She first displays her knowledge to Melanie by reeling off the Greek scientific names for the crow and blackbird species. Of course, this is the sort of superficial book learning that the ignorant mistake for knowledge: we do not know something just because we have given a name to it (a fallacy inherent in today's plethora of medical "syndromes"). This is a perennial tendency of the human mind—not just to label things, but to imagine that this labeling somehow removes their otherness and brings them under our control. It is a tendency that begins in Genesis 2:19: "And out of the ground the Lord God formed every beast of the field, and every fowl of the air; and brought them unto Adam to see what he would call them: and whatsoever Adam called every living creature, that was the name thereof."

Mrs. Bundy is, in fact, a droll parody of modern, Western, pig-headed "scientism." When she hears from Melanie that crows attacked the school, she is immediately dismissive: "I hardly think either species would have the intelligence to launch a massed attack. Their brain pans aren't large enough for such . . ." In other words, this proud empiricist knows *a priori* that what Melanie witnessed with her own eyes cannot have happened. Melanie responds, sensibly, "I just came from the school, madam. I don't know about their brain pans but . . ."

Mrs. Bundy cuts her off: "Well, I do." And she repeats this, emphatically: "I *do* know. Ornithology happens to be my avocation." Then she adopts a tone of warm condescension: "Birds are not aggressive creatures, Miss. They bring beauty into the world. It is mankind, rather, who . . ." She had been about to deliver an eloquent speech against man, on behalf of the birds. But the voice of mundane, common life intervenes: "Three Southern fried chicken, Sam! Baked potato on all of them!" It is the voice of the waitress calling to the cook. Mrs. Bundy shoots her an aggrieved look, then completes her thought: "who insists on making it difficult for life to survive on this planet. If it weren't for birds . . ."

How typical of Mrs. Bundy's type—to side with the birds over her own species. How very white of her. This time it is Deke who cuts her off. "Mrs. Bundy, you don't seem to understand. This young lady says there was an attack on the school." "Impossible!" cries Mrs. Bundy. Mere facts are insufficient to derail this old crone's relentless pursuit of the truth. The drunk at the end of the bar now cries "It's the end of the world!" Then he quotes scripture, before taking another swig of his beer. "Thus saith the Lord God to the mountains, and to the hills, to the rivers and to the valleys, behold, I, even I, will bring a sword upon you, and I will destroy your high places. In all your dwelling places, the cities shall be laid waste, and the high places shall be laid waste! Ezekiel, Chapter Six."

The man is drinking while Irish, so the audience is disposed not to take what he says seriously. Plus, he is quoting scripture, which for many modern people is a sign of ignorance and superstition. And yet, on another level we are bothered by what this man says. Everything has been turned upside down in *The Birds*. Nature, it seems, has turned on man—and why this is happening is so far unexplained (in fact, it will remain unexplained). The old and familiar is now unfamiliar and terrifying. Lives are on hold. The ways in which we are accustomed to understanding the world around us are being challenged. Perhaps nothing will ever be the same again. Perhaps it *really is* the end of the world, and this drunken Irishman is a prophet. In such times, people are tormented by the nagging thought that perhaps the old books and the old ways were right, and that maybe we are being punished for straying from them.

The drunken Irishman's rant is one element in a brilliant scene cleverly crafted to create an atmosphere of hysteria and impending doom. Mrs. Bundy, who is amused by the drunk, tries to reassure us: "I hardly think a few birds are going to bring about the end of the world." But Melanie, frustrated by the old lady's unwillingness to listen, counters, "These weren't a few birds."

The woman with the two children has been silent this whole time, but it is evident that she is becoming increasingly alarmed by these stories. She whispers to the waitress, "Could you ask them to lower their voices, please? They're frightening the children." Of course, as shall see, she is the one who is being most strongly affected by the conversation. The inclusion of this woman (who has some significant lines a little later) is another brilliant device to create tension. The presence of a person who is becoming increasingly nervous tends to make us nervous as well, like one tuning fork vibrating another. We begin to wonder whether we ought to be nervous also, and what this nervous person before us might do.

At this point, Mr. Sholes, the fisherman, tells the group about an incident from the previous week in which one of his boats was attacked by gulls. "Practically tore the skipper's arm off," he says. Deke mentions that Melanie was attacked by a gull two days earlier. Once again, Mrs. Bundy rides to the rescue. "The gulls were after your fish, Mr. Sholes," she says. "Really, let's be logical about this." But Melanie counters with the perfect response, "What were the crows after at the school?"

"What do you think they were after?" Mrs. Bundy asks. Hitchcock's camera now shows us closer shots of both characters, suggesting that this conversation is about to get intense. Melanie thinks for a moment, then says, "I think they were after the children." "For what purpose?" Mrs. Bundy asks. With some hesitation, Melanie answers,

"To kill them." She does not want to say this because she does not want to think it, but this is her honest view, and she is correct. Now there is an even tighter closeup of Mrs. Bundy as she simply says "Why?" Her tone is challenging, but there is something in her eyes that suggests apprehension. For some reason, this moment is chilling. "I don't know why," Melanie responds, and Mrs. Bundy is instantly relieved, and now more arrogant and dismissive than ever. "I thought not," she says, with evident satisfaction.

You see, according to Mrs. Bundy's "logic," if Melanie can't explain the attack on the children then it must not have happened. It is actually Melanie who is more logical than Mrs. Bundy, for she seeks the truth wherever it may lead, whereas Mrs. Bundy refuses to consider evidence. Why? Because it would overturn everything that she believes and shake her conviction that logic has revealed the world to her and brought it under her control. To paraphrase what D. H. Lawrence once said of Walt Whitman, Mrs. Bundy drives an automobile with a very fierce headlight, along the track of a fixed idea, through the darkness of this world. And she sees everything that way. Just as a motorist does in the night.[3]

"Birds have been on this planet since archaeopteryx," proclaims Mrs. Bundy. "A hundred and twenty million years ago! Doesn't it seem odd that they'd wait all that time to start a . . . a war against humanity?" Mrs. Bundy's worldview has no room for the anomalous, for the unpredicted, and certainly not for the inexplicable. The darkness unilluminated by her headlight is vast. Because she can't see it, it does not exist for her.

---

[3] D. H. Lawrence, "Whitman," *Studies in Classic American Literature* (London: Penguin, 1971), 175.

CHAPTER FOUR

In the Tides Restaurant scene, in Evan Hunter's original script, Melanie offers a suggestion as to why the birds have been attacking: "Maybe they're all protecting the species. Maybe they're tired of being shot at and roasted in ovens and . . ." This line was cut, however, in keeping with Hitchcock's desire to eliminate any explanation for the attacks. Since Melanie has so far been the most reasonable person in the scene, her suggestion would have carried weight with the audience—despite the fact that a sign in the restaurant looms over her saying "Absolutely No Credit." (There is actually a good bit of "flab" that was removed from Hunter's original version of the Tides scene.)

In the midst of the discussion between Melanie and the locals, in walks a travelling salesman: a grey man in a grey suit wearing a grey hat. A hard drinker and a world-weary cynic, he sits at the bar and orders a scotch and water ("light on the water"). The salesman listens in on the conversation about the birds then says with a snarl, "Get yourself guns and wipe them off the face of the earth." "That would hardly be possible," says Mrs. Bundy confidently. "Because there are eight thousand six hundred and fifty species of birds in the world today. It's estimated that five billion, seven hundred and fifty million birds live in the United States alone. The five continents of the world probably contain more than a hundred billion birds!" To this, the drunk at the end of the bar responds once more, "It's the end of the world!"

When Melanie mentions that different species of birds have been flocking together in some of these attacks (as in the one on the Brenner living room), Mrs. Bundy says emphatically, "I have never known birds of different species to flock together. The very concept is unimaginable! Why if that happened, we wouldn't have a chance. How could we possibly hope to fight them?" Aside from once more illustrating Mrs. Bundy's rigid "logic," these lines are calculated to bring the tension in the scene to a boil. It does indeed now seem like the end of the world—for, unlike Mrs. Bundy, *we* know that the bird attacks are real, and that this is just the beginning.

It is at this point that the nervous mother with the two children just can't take it anymore. "If that young lady saw an attack on the school, why won't you believe her?" she asks, sensibly. "You're all sitting around here debating! What do you want them to do next? Crash through that window?" She is on her way out of town and gets the salesman to agree to show her how to get to the freeway. Mitch now enters, having come from the Fawcett farm. The Santa Rosa police think Fawcett was killed by a burglar—yet another howler from our highly logical species. "Were the Santa Rosa police at your school today?" says the nervous woman, again asking the right questions. Aside from Mrs. Bundy, it is actually the women in this film who are quickest to understand what they are all really facing.

The salesman now mentions that he recalls something similar happening in Santa Cruz the previous year. Seagulls got lost in the fog and swept into the town, making a terrible mess. "The point is that no one seemed to get upset about it," says Mrs. Bundy. "They were gone the next morning, just as if nothing at all had happened. Poor things." Here Hunter's script refers to an actual incident that took place in Santa Cruz in 1961. It was this incident, plus another like it in La Jolla in 1960, plus Daphne du Maurier's short story "The Birds" that jointly provided the inspiration for the film.

The salesman finally finishes his drink and departs, closely followed by the mother and her two children.

Mitch now corners Sebastian Sholes. "I think we're in trouble," Mitch says, as Melanie and the others listen. "I don't know how or why this started, but I know it's here, and I know we'd be crazy to ignore it." "Ignore what? The bird war?" asks Mrs. Bundy, her voice dripping with sarcasm. At this point Mitch explodes at her: "Yes, the bird war, the bird attack, the bird plague, you can call it what you want to, they're out there massing someplace and they'll be back, you can count on that!" "Ridiculous," Mrs. Bundy snaps, and in the script (but not in the finished film) Mitch responds, "Mrs. Bundy, why don't you go home and polish your binoculars?"

It soon becomes apparent, however, that Sholes cannot be counted on. Incredibly, he does not believe there's a crisis either, even after hearing all the evidence, including's Mitch's report about what happened at the Fawcett farm. Sholes does not believe because, as he says, "I can't see any reason for it." Mitch's response is significant. He says, "It's happening. Isn't that a good enough reason?" Both Sholes and Mrs. Bundy reject the reality of the bird attacks not just because they "can't see any reason" for them, but because the attacks conflict with what they already believe to be true. Not just about birds, but about human knowledge. Both characters exhibit the modern tendency to overestimate our ability to know and to control nature. Their worldview does not admit the possibility of mystery.

This now seems as good as any place to bring in Heidegger (who has been waiting in the wings for some time) and to discuss what is, for me, the major point of the film.

The Birds is a film about what Heidegger calls *das Ereignis*. This common German word is usually translated as "the event." Heidegger uses the term, however, in a very uncommon way, drawing on its etymology (which I will save for the following chapter) and also insisting that it should *not* be understood as "event." Against Heidegger's wishes, however, we *can* understand *Ereignis* as an "event," though of a very special kind. As Greg Johnson notes, *Ereignis* refers to "fundamental transformations of *the meaning of everything*, such as the emergence of modernity—or its replacement with something else."[1]

Ereignis is a change in how a culture understands the being of beings. Put more simply (too simply, I'm sure, for Heidegger scholars), *Ereignis* is a change in how we understand, in a fundamental sense, *what things are*. Needless to say, we have always known that such shifts take place. We know that our modern way of understanding what things are is markedly different from that of, say, Christendom in the High Middles Ages, or that of Homeric Greece.

So is Heidegger saying anything new here? He is indeed, for at least in the modern period we believe that human beings *themselves* bring about these shifts in being, through "advances" in scientific and philosophical thinking, and through conscious choice. Such a position makes mankind master of its destiny, as the supreme author of the cultures it lives under. Heidegger calls this position "humanism," and he rejects it completely. Heidegger is an arch *anti*-humanist, and this is the foundation of his conservatism. In fact, I would argue that true conservatism is essentially identical with anti-humanism.

Heidegger notes that while we moderns *theorize* that historical change is due to conscious human thought and decision (as in the notion that philosophers are the "hidden legislators" of mankind), our actual *experience* of our relationship to history is markedly different. As Johnson notes, further:

---

[1] Greg Johnson, "Heidegger without Being," *Counter-Currents*, April 2, 2020.

When individuals reflect upon language, culture, and history, we experience them as things that existed before our consciousness emerged, as things that will continue to exist after our consciousness has ended, and as external forces that envelope and enthrall us. They do stand over against us as objects—and also behind us as conditions of our subjectivity.[2]

Indeed, we are not, as individuals or as a group, the masters of these conditions. Rather, they master us. As a simple illustration of this, just think of all the people around us who are in thrall to the modern, liberal *Zeitgeist*—without, for the most part, being aware of it. Think of the countless people who intone the slogan "diversity is our strength," as if they think it was their own personal coinage. Then consider your own sense of detachment from that *Zeitgeist*.[3] "Surely," you think to yourself, "I have transcended my historical situation; surely, I am in control." Until, inevitably, you are brought face to face now and then with the ways in which you are very much a product of your time, and always will be.

"But surely," one may persist, "some people *really are* the authors of major cultural change; change in how we understand what things are. Admittedly, it is not I. It is men like Descartes, who brought about a sea change in Western thought, and helped create the modern mind." To this, Heidegger would respond that men like Descartes are merely articulating a change in the *Zeitgeist* that was

---

[2] Greg Johnson, "*Making Sense of Heidegger*," *Counter-Currents*, December 12, 2014.

[3] The term *Zeitgeist*, "spirit of the times," is usually associated with Hegel, but we can still use this term in understanding Heidegger. Hegel's own peculiar use of it is not intended here.

underway before they ever set pen to paper. This is why Descartes was so enthusiastically received by so many: he came along "at the right time." We critics of modernity are in the same boat: not bringing about the death of modernity, but heralding it, like Nietzsche's Madman, or Hegel's Owl of Minerva, which takes flight only at dusk. In every case, the great minds give expression to a change in the *Zeitgeist* they did not themselves initiate—something that was, as we say, "in the air." But how did the change actually get underway? What is the something that was "in the air"? And what is the something that is metaphorically expressed as "the air"?

For Heidegger, these questions simply cannot be answered. The reason is that, at any given time, our way of making sense of things, of understanding what things are, is conditioned by whatever the *Zeitgeist* happens to be. That *Zeitgeist*, that "epoch of being" serves as the "horizon" (to use Heideggerese) within which we make sense of things. We are all born within a "worldview," and I can no more get out from under it than, as Hegel said, a man can jump over the Colossus of Rhodes. But if it is only *within* such a horizon that we can make sense out of things, then where that (or any) horizon has come from, or how it has come, is ultimately unintelligible.

This amounts to anti-humanism and anti-modernism, essentially because Heidegger is saying that we are not the masters of our own fate. As human beings we are fated to try to make sense out of things (as Aristotle said "all men by nature desire to know"). Yet exactly *why* this is and why we make sense out of things in the way we do, in any given epoch of being, remains a mystery to us. All that we can say is that human life is moved by factors that are never fully clear to us, and will remain so. We are not in control, though we have a built-in tendency to imagine that we are.

This tendency is not itself modern. The Greeks knew

about it, and they had a word for it: *hubris*. Essentially, modernity is the age of hubris. An age in which men could build a gigantic ship, christen it "Titanic" (after the Titans, who challenged the gods), and declare it "unsinkable"—all apparently without anyone suggesting at some point that perhaps this wasn't such a good idea. Our pre-modern ancestors were proto-Heideggerians: they understood that their minds illuminated only a small portion of what is, and that much else will always remain a mystery, including the conditions that make possible human knowing itself.

What we have in *The Birds* is a Heideggerian "Event": a sudden and fundamental transformation of the meaning of everything. It comes out of nowhere. It completely upends life as we know it. And *why* it comes is inexplicable. Before the bird attacks, we were all Mrs. Bundy: we thought we had this world figured out. Why, we knew the Greek and Latin scientific names for everything! We had established that nature behaves according to regularities, which we christened "laws." This essentially involves thinking that nature *cannot* behave in any way other than how we expect it to. (For more information, consult David Hume.)

Further, we imagined that our limited knowledge had put us in control of nature; that what our ancestors struggled against had now been tamed and would never bother us again. So we settled into a comfortable complacency, sleepwalking through trivial and aimless lives, like Melanie's "jobs" and practical jokes. We became self-absorbed, never really committing or living for anything (Mitch's womanizing; Annie's dead-end spinsterhood in Bodega Bay; Lydia's fear of abandonment). Death itself seemed unreal, something that happened to other people, or that could be kept at bay through pills or diets or hormones. So why the hurry? Why *do* anything?

But into the land of these lotus eaters come the birds,

who change the meaning of everything. Our former way of understanding the being of things—what nature is and what it is capable of; what *we* are and what *we* are capable of—is completely invalidated the moment that gull strikes Melanie on the head. In an interview conducted at the time of the film's release, Hitchcock was asked what the film is "about." He answered as follows:

> Generally speaking, that people are too complacent. The girl [i.e., Melanie] represents complacency. But I believe that when people rise to the occasion, when catastrophe comes, they are all right. The mother panics because she starts off being so strong, but she is not strong, it is a facade: she has been substituting her son for her husband. She is the weak character in the story. But the girl shows that people can be strong when they face up to the situation. It's like the people in London, during the wartime air raids.[4]

My own interpretation of the film is completely compatible with that of its director. I am simply digging down to a deeper complacency—the complacency of modernity itself. Hitchcock's "catastrophe" is equivalent to my Heideggerian use of "event." "Catastrophe" is a Greek noun, derived from *katastrepho*, "I overturn." The prefix *kata-* can mean against, back, or downwards, while *strepho* means "to twist." Together, they mean something like "twist against" or "twist back down." The sense of a reversal is implied, so that "overturn" is a decent translation. Such an "overturning" is exactly what humanity, represented by our cast of very imperfect characters, under-

---

[4] Alfred Hitchcock, Interview on *The Birds*, 1963, online at https://www.moma.org/interactives/exhibitions/1999/hitchcoc k/interview/interview_10.html

goes in *The Birds*.

In his comments, Hitchcock puts the focus on what becomes of the characters as a result of this overturning. I shall argue in a later chapter that, in fact, the only sense of "resolution" in the film comes in the form of definite indications that the characters develop and grow. But if we ask about the larger effects of the Event, about what it will bring for humanity as a whole (if, indeed, the bird attacks are a global phenomenon), then there is simply no answer to this.

When the Event comes, we cannot know exactly what it will issue in. We do not predict it and we do not control it, so we cannot know what its outcome will be for us; we cannot know how being will change. Hitchcock signifies this, notoriously, by ending the film (*spoiler alert!*) without any resolution to the story at all. We never learn why the birds attack, whether it remains a localized phenomenon (I will argue that it does not), and what happens to the main characters.

I should mention here that of course I am not saying that Hitchcock was familiar with Heidegger, or even that he was consciously trying to make larger philosophical points in the film. I don't even fundamentally care what Hitchcock himself thought of the film (though what he says is, as we have seen, helpful). Works of art mean more than their authors intend. This is the case for at least two reasons. First, as culture changes, as the horizon of meaningfulness changes, the meaning an artwork has for audiences changes as well. Second, an artwork is at least partly a projection of the artist's subconscious mind. I believe this is especially true of Hitchcock's films, which were the product of a highly intelligent but deeply repressed personality.

At first blush, one might think this means that an artwork would only give us an indication of the artist's own peculiar psychology. But this misses the obvious fact that the author is a member of the human species. In addition to whatever may be peculiarly his own, he also expresses preoccupations, desires, aspirations, and anxieties that may resonate with all men, or at least all men in the artist's own culture milieu. In general, when I interpret a film, I follow the advice of D. H. Lawrence:

> The artist usually sets out—or used to—to point a moral and adorn a tale. The tale, however, points the other way, as a rule. Two blankly opposing morals, the artist's and the tale's. Never trust the artist. Trust the tale. The proper function of a critic is to save the tale from the artist who created it.[5]

Despite this, I do believe that, setting Heideggerian lingo aside, I am not actually "reading something into" *The Birds* that is not actually there. This is a film that demands repeated viewings and handsomely repays the effort one puts into it. Intelligent viewers who have never read Heidegger can see that this is a film about empty, modern, complacent lives overturned and transformed by an encounter with mystery. It is deeply anti-modern, and anti-humanist. And I do not believe for a moment that this was entirely something "subconscious" on the part of the filmmakers. Characters like Mrs. Bundy don't just happen by accident.

We can come to a deeper understanding of the filmmakers' intentions by examining the work of one contributor who has so far not been mentioned, production designer Robert Boyle. Boyle had previously worked with Hitchcock on *Saboteur* (1942) and *North by Northwest* (1959). On *The Birds*, Hitchcock sought Boyle's input before Evan Hunter was ever engaged to write the screenplay. Hitchcock had Boyle read Daphne du Maurier's short

---

[5] D. H. Lawrence, *Studies in Classic American Literature*, 8.

story and produce some sketches to establish a possible "look" for the film. Boyle's initial sketches depict a single episode in the story, in which the main character and his daughter are attacked by birds while on their way home.[6] Boyle's inspiration for these images, and throughout all his subsequent work on the film, was, surprisingly, Edvard Munch's 1893 painting *The Scream*.

Munch's most celebrated composition, *The Scream* exists in several versions: two in paint, two in pastel, and several prints from a lithograph stone created by the artist. The image has a curious power to become the object of obsession, and over the years both of the paintings have been stolen, then recovered. In 2012 one of the pastels fetched a record $120 million when it was auctioned at Sotheby's.

Like Hitchcock, Munch poured his own darkest obsessions into his artwork, and *The Scream* is probably the finest example in art history of an attempt to express a psychological state in a single image. Madness ran in Munch's family, and he grew up with the fear that it would one day take him over. Munch did indeed suffer a nervous breakdown in 1908, but after eight months of confinement to a psychiatric clinic he seemed to make a full recovery.

At some point, Munch came under the influence of the Norwegian nihilist and anarchist Hans Jaeger who lived by the credo "a passion to destroy is also a creative passion." Jaeger encouraged Munch to depict his own psychological states, from which emerged what Munch would call his "soul paintings," the most celebrated of which is *The Scream*. Munch wrote the following about the origins of the painting, which was conceived in Oslo (then called Kristiania):

---

[6] For the sketches, see the online version of this chapter, Derek Hawthorne, "*The Birds*, Part 4," *Counter-Currents*, June 1, 2020.

I was walking down the road with two friends when the sun set; suddenly, the sky turned as red as blood. I stopped and leaned against the fence, feeling unspeakably tired. Tongues of fire and blood stretched over the bluish black fjord. My friends went on walking, while I lagged behind, shivering with fear. Then I heard the enormous, infinite scream of nature.

The painting has frequently been interpreted as an expression of modern "existential angst." Munch later said, "for several years I was almost mad. . . . You know my picture, *The Scream*? I was stretched to the limit—nature was screaming in my blood. . . . After that I gave up hope ever of being able to love again."

What motivated Boyle's choice of *The Scream* as inspiration for *The Birds*? Since the screenplay was not yet written, we have to look to the content of the Du Maurier story for answers. Doing so also allows us to comment on the continuity between the story and the film—something which is seldom perceived, since the plots and characters of the two are markedly different.

The short story focusses on one family, a farmer with his wife and two children, living in rural England. Suddenly one evening, birds begin attacking their house. This is dismissed as a fluke, until the attacks continue. At one point, a visit to a nearby farmhouse results in the discovery of the corpses of a man and his wife killed by birds (the inspiration for the Fawcett farm sequence in the film). The climax of the story involves the family waiting out the bird attacks in their boarded-up house, fending off attempts by the birds to breach their fortifications—including one episode in which the birds come down the chimney, just as in the film. Also just like the film, the story ends without any resolution. We do not find out what becomes of the family, and the reason for the bird attacks is never explained.

A general feeling of despair and helplessness hangs over the tale. The farmer, whose name is Nat, thinks at one point, "Someone should know of this. Someone should be told. Something was happening, because of the east wind and the weather, that he did not understand. He wondered if he should go to the callbox by the bus stop and ring up the police. Yet what could they do? What could anyone do?"[7] Listening to "the wireless," however, the family learns that the bird attacks have spread to the entire country. This convinces Nat that it is only a matter of time before the men he looks up to as authorities come riding to the rescue. He thinks to himself:

> "There's one thing, the best brains of the country will be onto it tonight." Somehow the thought reassured him. He had a picture of scientists, naturalists, technicians, and all those chaps they called the backroom boys, summoned to a council; they'd be working on the problem now. This was not a job for the government, for the chiefs-of-staff—they would merely carry out the orders of the scientists.[8]

His wife has an even greater faith in authority figures (as most women do), and wonders why they fail to act: "Why don't the authorities do something? Why don't they get the army, get machine guns, anything?" She even says at one point, "Won't America do something? . . . They've always been our allies, haven't they? Surely America will do something?"[9] But du Maurier instead shows that human beings, especially trusted authorities, prove com-

---

[7] Daphne du Maurier, *The Birds and Other Stories* (London: Virago Press, 2004), 11.

[8] Du Maurier, *The Birds*, 25.

[9] Du Maurier, *The Birds*, 38.

pletely incapable not just of understanding what is happening and doing something about it, but even of accepting *that* it is happening.

Eventually, the authorities do act, but the result is disastrous. The RAF are called into action, but their planes crash when they fly into the great flocks of birds that hang over the country like angry clouds. "What could aircraft do against birds that flung themselves to death against propeller and fuselage, but hurtle to the ground themselves?" Nat thinks to himself, "Someone high up had lost his head."[10] The authorities have completely failed—both the authority of government, and the authority of what had been "settled" knowledge of the universe. In the end, the characters are completely abandoned, left alone to face the very real possibility of death, unaided by comforting illusions. Arguably, this is as "existentialist" a story as anything by Camus.

And we can definitely discern a continuity of mood and themes between story and film. The bird attacks are "absurd" in the sense that they defy our attempts to make them intelligible. This brings us face to face with our own hubris in thinking that we have made the physical universe fully transparent to us, and manipulable. Our helplessness in the face of the terrifying power of the Unknown is exposed. And we might as well identify Nature with the Unknown, for what *The Birds* suggests is that the greater part of nature is unknown, the huge underside of the proverbial iceberg, the part that sinks our titanic pretensions.

It seems clear that Robert Boyle, who was a highly cultivated man, perceived the "existentialist" themes in du Maurier's story, and made an intuitive connection to Munch's *The Scream*, which, as already noted, is widely interpreted as a portrait of "existential angst." Although

---

[10] Du Maurier, *The Birds*, 25.

the sketches Boyle initially produced, inspired by Munch, depict a scene that does not make it into the film, *The Scream* remained his inspiration throughout the design of the picture. This is especially the case with the depiction of the skyline around Bodega Bay. Grey, overcast skies were painted in by matte artist Albert Whitlock, to give the setting an ominous feeling of impending doom.[11]

It was Boyle himself who found Bodega Bay when scouting locations and proposed it to Hitchcock as a suitably "bleak" location for the film. It is thus clear that at least some of the personnel involved with the film were aware of the story's philosophical depth even if it remained, for them, on the level of mood and atmosphere rather than some sort of articulated "message." It is also fortuitous that Munch characterized the psychological state expressed in *The Scream* as the result of hearing "the enormous, infinite scream of nature." This scream of nature is, of course, what the film depicts, though it would be a stretch to insist that Boyle was aware of this quote from Munch.

In the next chapter, we will examine the question of what it means to call *The Birds* an "apocalyptic film"—a description many have endorsed. We will consider what Heidegger would have called the "originary meaning" of the Greek *apocalypsis*.

---

[11] Tony Lee Moral writes that, "expressionistic art was at the very heart of the film's conception" (Moral, *The Making of Hitchcock's* The Birds, 71). Although Whitlock also drew inspiration from the paintings of John Constable and William Turner, especially Constable's 1821 painting *The Hay Wain*. See Moral, 93.

CHAPTER FIVE

Let us now consider more closely some of Hitchcock's explicit statements about the meaning of *The Birds*. In the same interview quoted in the last chapter, film critic Peter Bogdanovich (who later became a director himself) asks "Isn't the film also a vision of Judgment Day?" Hitchcock responds:

> Yes, it is. And we don't know how they are going to come out. Certainly, the mother was scared to the end. The girl was brave enough to face the birds and try to beat them off. But as a group they were the victims of Judgment Day. For the ordinary public— they got away to San Francisco—but I toyed with the idea of lap-dissolving on them in the car, looking, and there is the Golden Gate Bridge—covered in birds.

What exactly does Hitchcock mean here by "Judgment Day"? This is a common, loose way of referring to the events described in the apocalyptic passages in the Bible. A Google search for "'Hitchcock' 'The Birds' 'apocalyptic'" returns more than fifty-two thousand results. The first is a 2012 article on *The Birds* from *The Guardian*, at the end of which a commentator quotes Fellini describing the film as "an apocalyptic tone poem." (The commentator responds, "that gets it about right.") Describing *The Birds* as "apocalyptic" is indeed very popular, and it is intuitively correct. A consideration of what exactly "the apocalypse" is will deepen our understanding of the film and will complement what has already been said about Heidegger and Munch.

Let us approach the subject, in fact, as Heidegger himself would, by considering the etymology of "apocalypse." The word is Greek, *apocalypsis*. *Apo-* is a versatile prefix in Classical Greek, but it can mean un- (as in undoing, unclean, unable), and linguists take it to mean this in *apocalypsis*. The rest of the word is derived from *kalypto*, "I cover" (the name of the Homeric Calypso comes from this, and basically means "she who conceals"). Thus, *apocalypsis* literally means "uncovering." It is more often translated "revelation" (which, of course, literally means uncovering), hence "The Revelation of John" ("Book of Revelation"), the Greek title for which is *Apocalypsis Ioannou*, or simply *Apocalypsis*.

This is grist for Heidegger's mill if ever there was, since it means that apocalypse has more or less the same meaning as the Greek *alētheia*, which is usually translated as "truth" but which Heidegger analyzes as meaning "uncovering" or "unconcealment." *Alētheia* is a crucially important word for Heidegger, but strangely he did not seem to make the connection to *apocalypsis* (at least, so far as I know). An apocalypse is thus a revelation or unconcealment of some truth, which had hitherto been veiled from human sight.[1]

Heidegger's own terminology is fraught with problems: peculiar choices of words (which often do not actually mean what they seem to mean), inconsistent usage, and, perhaps most bothersome of all, the introduction of multiple terms that seem to all wind up meaning the same thing. In Heidegger's philosophy, "unconcealment" is ultimately equivalent to what he calls "the clearing" (*die Lichtung*). This a metaphor. Heidegger is thinking of a clearing in a forest, which allows light to enter in. Thomas

---

[1] See Thomas Sheehan for a discussion of why *alētheia* should not be translated as "truth." Thomas Sheehan, *Making Sense of Heidegger: A Paradigm Shift* (Lanham, Maryland: Rowman and Littlefield, 2014), 61–62.

Sheehan describes the clearing as "the always already opened-up 'space' that makes the being of things (phenomenologically: the intelligibility of things) possible and necessary."[2] The usually lucid Sheehan fails us a bit here, since his definition repeats the spatial metaphor present in the language of clearing (and putting "space" in quotes is not a solution).

Nonetheless, the concept of the clearing is not that difficult to understand. Suppose I am walking through the hills of Sonoma County and on the horizon I see a tall, skinny object which I cannot immediately identify. I approach closer and see that it is a scarecrow standing in someone's field. The object has now become meaningful to me. We can also use the language of being and say that I have now registered *what* the object *is*. On one level, this seems like an active process. Perhaps, as I advance closer to the unidentified object, I am racking my brain, going over the different options for what this thing might be. But when I actually see that it is a scarecrow, it is as if the "scarecrowness" of this object just suddenly "appears" for me, "overlaying" the now-identified object.

I don't *experience* this as an act of actively imposing some idea or schema of "scarecrowness" onto an object. Instead, the experience I have is that the being or meaning of the object, its "scarecrowness," *comes to meet me*. For this to be possible, for the being or meaning of objects to display itself to me, I must possess a certain sort of "openness" in which this can happen. Again, I do not experience myself as slapping a meaning onto an object: I experience that meaning as something that, in a sense "comes forth" in my awareness, because I have made myself open to receive this. To use Sheehan's language, my awareness, my openness creates a kind of "space" in which the meaning of things can show up to me. Heidegger's metaphorical

---

[2] Sheehan, *Making Sense of Heidegger*, 20.

language for this is straightforward: a clearing in the forest (= my subjective "openness") allows light (= meaning/being) to enter in, revealing things to me in this light.

Here is another example: suppose I pick up an unfamiliar object from Annie Hayworth's coffee table. I roll it around in my hand, baffled as to what it is. I am in a state of suspense: what it is will not reveal itself to me. It looks kind of like a rock, but it clearly isn't. So I keep on exploring the object. I fumble open what turns out to be a hinged top—and then, all of a sudden, it hits me: this is a cigarette lighter.

Yes, I suppose it's plausible to say that I have "fitted" the object within "mental categories," based on prior knowledge. This may sound like a hardheaded description of the "mechanism" involved but note that it is entirely metaphorical. Let's dispense with attempts to describe what is happening behind the scenes and just *describe my experience*—which is what phenomenology does. If I do this, then, to be faithful to that experience I must note that the being or meaning of the object seems to just *emerge* at a certain point. It is almost irresistible to have recourse to more metaphors here—to speak of the being of the thing as suddenly "shining forth," or some such. (This should cause us to feel some sympathy for Heidegger's struggles with language.)

The real point is that if I were not, in some fundamental sense, "open" to the display of the being of things, then I would never be able to say "Oh, that's a scarecrow" or "That's a cigarette lighter." Nit pickers will charge that I have just substituted one metaphor for another: just as Sheehan replaced Heidegger's "clearing" with "space," so I have replaced Sheehan's "space" with "openness." In fact, I am not so sure that "openness" is metaphorical here, but to discuss that point would take us too far afield.

So far so good. Unconcealment (*alētheia*, "truth") is equivalent to the clearing. In the clearing we register what things are or what they mean. Perhaps, as I approached that object in the field, I thought it was a man, only to get closer and register that it is actually a scarecrow. So does that mean that what is "unconcealed" in the clearing is what things *truly* are? Their true being?

Not so fast. We are tempted to say this, but remember what was discussed in the previous chapter: things are always meaningful to us (i.e., they show up as beings of a certain sort) within a horizon of meaning that is historically conditioned. (What I loosely referred to in chapter four as a *Zeitgeist*.) This means that the being of things changes over time. What we take things to be or to mean changes over the course of history.[3]

But can a scarecrow ever cease to be a scarecrow? Yes and no. When I see the thing I say, "there's a scarecrow," but I take it quite differently from someone living a hundred years ago. Back then, a scarecrow was merely a utilitarian object. When I see it, however, I see a relic of a bygone age, the age of small farming. (Agribusiness doesn't need scarecrows; its terrible machines keep the birds away.) "Isn't that quaint?" I say. On further investigation, I might find the scarecrow is in that field precisely because the owner's wife thinks it is quaint and decorative. I may also think of the scarecrow in *The Wizard of Oz*, or of any number of horror films.

It is the same with the tabletop cigarette lighter. No longer exclusively a utilitarian object, it is now a display of postmodern "hipster" irony, like Tiki mugs and vinyl and fabulous fifties furniture (take a closer look at Annie Hay-

---

[3] Sheehan persuasively argues that Heidegger uses the terms "being" and "meaning" synonymously. If you object to this and insist that a thing's being (what it *is*) is not reducible to what it means *to us*, then I would invite you to go in search of what "being" actually means. You'll be on that journey for a long time.

worth's living room for an unironic display of classic
style). It also symbolizes, for me and many others, a world
well lost: a world of rank odors and hacking coughs and
lung surgeons with nicotine-stained hands. This is all now
a part of what the object *means*, a part of its being—but
that wasn't true fifty or sixty years ago.

This means that there is a close connection between
what Heidegger calls the clearing, in which the being of
things shows up for us, and what he calls *das Ereignis*, the
Event. Recall that the Event is a sudden and fundamental
transformation of the meaning of everything. But what
makes possible the meaningfulness of things is the clearing. Thus, the Event is a transformation in the clearing,
and this transformation is "historical," in the sense that it
is a change in cultural meaning undergone by a people.
This makes it possible for Heidegger to speak of "epochs
of being." With the Event, *how* things become meaningful
to us within the clearing changes in truly *fundamental*
ways. A new "age" is born, marked by a new way of understanding the being/meaning of beings.

I noted earlier that "apocalypse" has roughly the same
literal meaning as *alētheia*—uncovering, or unconcealment—and that this is also equivalent to Heidegger's
Lichtung, clearing. That is correct insofar as the *literal*
meaning of apocalypse goes, but the *connotations* of
apocalypse and uncovering/unconcealment are nonetheless different.

This is obvious if we consider the Latinate translation
of apocalypse: revelation. A "revelation" is not just any old
"uncovering of meaning." The sense of "Revelation" has
four aspects: it is (1) the uncovering of some ultimate,
world-shaking (or ego-shaking) meaning, that is (2) ab-
rupt, sudden, and usually unanticipated, (3) not under our
control, and (4) radically transformative: once it occurs,
nothing will be the same again. Thus, apocalypse = the
Event.

To delve more deeply into this equivalency, and thus more deeply into the meaning of *The Birds*, let us now consider Heidegger's peculiar etymology of *Ereignis*. Thomas Sheehan sums things up neatly:

> Heidegger understands *Ereignis* in terms of its etymological roots, which go back to the German word for "eye." The brothers Grimm had demonstrated that the original etymon of *Ereignis* is the Old High German *ouga*, "eye" (see the modern German *Auge*). *Ouga* underlies the Old High German verb *ir-ougen* and the Middle High German *er-öugen* and *er-äugen*, as well as the obsolete High German verb *er-eigen*, all of which mean "to place before the eyes, to show," parallel to the Latin verbs *monstrare* and *ostendere*. Over the centuries, however, the etymology shifted significantly as the entirely unrelated adjective *eigen* ("one's own") and its cognate verb *an-eigen* ("to appropriate") came to be associated with *sich er-eigen*. Eventually the two meanings—on the one hand, "to eye something," and on the other, "to own it"—got commingled. Furthermore, by the early 1600s the letter *n* crept in (as in *sich er-eignen*).[4]

Heidegger plays on both of these etymological source meanings of *Ereignis*: "to see" and "to own/appropriate." (It is for this reason that some Heidegger translators make life difficult for us by rendering *Ereignis* as "appropriation" or "the Event of appropriation" or even, God help us, "enowning.") In the second sense of "to own/appropriate," the Event is "our own" in that it constitutes our own human being. I do not create the Event, I undergo it. But the undergoing of the Event and the making meaningful of things within the historically conditioned clearing is what

---

[4] Sheehan, *Making Sense of Heidegger*, 232.

it means to be human. The Event is thus "mine" and yet "not mine": my being stands over against me as something I must continually enact. To be human is to continually "open a space" in which the meaning of things comes to light. As Sheehan says, "*Ereignis* means that ex-sistence [*Dasein*, i.e., human nature] has always already been brought into its own as the thrown-open clearing, and 'occurs' precisely *as* that."[5]

However, it is the other "root meaning" of *Ereignis* that interests me more: "to see." Sheehan notes that Heidegger "hears in Ereignis echoes of '*in den Augen fallen . . . erscheinen.*'"[6] Sheehan correctly translates this quotation as "to come into view, to appear." But a barbarously (but helpfully) literal translation would be "to fall into the eyes, to shine out."[7] This neatly coincides with our suggestion that the Event is the same thing as the apocalypse, where the latter is a "revelation" or a "seeing."

"Seeing" is frequently referred to in Evan Hunter's screenplay. "See," "seeing," or "seen" occurs one hundred and forty-two times, sometimes in dialogue and some-times in Hunter's directions. Characters say "I see" eleven times. Characters say "you see" (sometimes "you'll see") fifteen times. "See," and variations, occurs on more than twenty other occasions in dialogue. Often, "seeing" is used in the sense of "knowing." For example, when Lydia first meets Melanie and learns that she has brought Mitch the lovebirds, she pointedly says "I see," and the screenplay describes her as "understanding completely now." Sebas-tian Sholes expresses skepticism about the "bird war," say-

---

[5] Sheehan, *Making Sense of Heidegger*, 234.

[6] Sheehan, *Making Sense of Heidegger*, 233.

[7] *Scheinen* is obviously cognate with "shine." The German prefix *er-* is hard to translate but it usually suggests a success-ful conclusion or outcome. Thus, *erscheinen* can be translated literally as "shining out," with the connotation that the shining or appearing is successfully or completely expressed.

ing to Mitch, "I can't see any reason for it."

Characters say "You know" (and sometimes, but not often, "You don't know") thirty-six times. "I know" (and a fair number of times "I don't know") is said thirty-four times. One of the most significant of these occasions is when Melanie confesses to Mrs. Bundy that she does not have any scientific knowledge of birds, to which Mrs. Bundy responds, "Well, I do. I *do* know."

As I've noted in earlier chapters, lack of vision, the inability to "see" or understand, and blindness are recurring themes in the film. The children at Cathy's party are attacked while playing blind man's bluff. Dan Fawcett's eyes are pecked out. One of the schoolchildren being chased by the crows falls and Hitchcock shows us a closeup of her thick eyeglasses smashed on the pavement. In scenes to come, one major character will be blinded, and birds will attempt to blind another.

Several characters are metaphorically blind to the peril posed by the birds—including the sheriff, Mrs. Bundy, and Sebastian Sholes. The characters who do recognize the crisis (Melanie, Mitch, Annie, and Lydia) are, at the same time, blind to the ways in which their own lives are stunted. However, as I shall argue, this blindness is cured when their eyes are opened to the enormity of the crisis that faces them, and, as a result, those characters grow.

In chapter one, I noted the "Oedipal" nature of Mitch's relationship to his mother, which is even referred to in dialogue. As I noted, however, the breaking of the incest taboo is not the major point of Sophocles's play. The events that lead to Oedipus's discovery that he has killed his father and married his own mother involve him seeking to know why a plague is ravaging Thebes.

The oracle at Delphi informs Creon, Oedipus's brother-in-law, that the plague is the result of the defilement of the city, given that the murderer of King Laius was never caught (that murderer is actually Oedipus, who killed Laius on the road, not knowing he was his father). Oedipus curses the murderer and makes a vow to discover his identity.

For advice, he calls in the prophet Tiresias, who happens to be blind. Tiresias has all the information Oedipus is seeking, but initially refuses to speak. This enrages Oedipus, who verbally assaults the prophet. In response, Tiresias reveals that Oedipus himself is the criminal he seeks. When the king mocks Tiresias's blindness, the prophet retorts, "You have your eyesight, but you do not see."

What is Oedipus's "tragic flaw"? It is actually not that obvious. On one level, it is clear that he is blind to the truth about his situation, and that he is the apparent cause of the plague. But what *really* causes the tragic events that follow—the suicide of his wife and mother, and Oedipus blinding himself and going into exile—is Oedipus's *desire to see*.

Tiresias actually advises him to give up his search, implying that some things are best *not known*. But Oedipus persists, with terrible results. His real blindness consists in not perceiving the limits of knowledge, or the unintended consequences of its relentless pursuit. To punish himself for *this* blindness, Oedipus blinds himself literally.

In *The Birds*, human beings are punished for this exact same blindness. Their unseeing eyes are attacked by the birds, and their lives turned upside down. At the same time, however, they are given a new vision: a revelation, an apocalypse, that ushers in a new "epoch of being" (though what that will be is not made clear in the film, which, as already noted, ends without any real resolution).

The "epoch of being" most fully discussed by Heidegger was post-war modernity, the essence of which he identifies as *das Gestell*. This is a common German word that is often translated as "rack" or "frame." Of course, as always, Heidegger uses the word in an uncommon way, and translators have struggled to express what he means. Often, they have translated *Gestell* as "enframing." Once again, Sheehan can serve as a reliable guide. He eschews a literal translation and interprets Gestell as "the world of exploitation." Sheehan explains this as follows:

> Heidegger reads the current dispensation [of being/the clearing] as one that provokes and even compels us to treat everything in terms of its exploitability-for-consumption: the being of things is now their ability to be turned into products for use and enjoyment. . . . Heidegger claims that in the modern world of calculative rationality, the instruments of technology and the mind-set of [*Technik*] dominate the way we understand and relate to everything. Earth is now seen as a vast storehouse of resources, both human and natural; and the value and realness of those resources, their being, is measured exclusively by their availability for consumption. Things are viewed, at least tacitly, as first and foremost *producenda et consumenda*, stuff to be exploited for commercialization and use. Their significance is measured by the degree to which they can be owned, stockpiled, marketed, sold, and consumed. And in a perverse phenomenological correlation, human beings are valued only for their ability to extract, work, shop, and consume. Exploitability for production and consumption has become the "truth" . . . of things, the dominant way they are now disclosed and will continue to be disclosed for the foreseeable future.[8]

It is not that difficult to see why Heidegger chooses *Gestell* to convey this modern mindset. It is as if we

---

[8] Sheehan, *Making Sense of Heidegger*, 258–59.

stretch the earth and everything on it on a rack, or "frame" everything in such a way that, so far as we are concerned, to be means to be raw material for human consumption and manipulation (what Heidegger calls *Bestand*, "stockpile," or, as translators usually render it, "standing-reserve"). Think of Procrustes and his bed.

It is the epoch of being as "enframing" that is negated in *The Birds*. In a 1963 interview with a French journalist,[9] Hitchcock stated that the theme of *The Birds* "is that man must be responsible to nature. He cannot assume that nature is always beneficial." (What Hitchcock probably meant here was "beneficent.") He adds, "The beautiful scenery, the sea and the sky, the trees, everything he enjoys." In other words, modern man has reduced nature to a pleasing backdrop, to "beautiful scenery" that exists to be consumed and enjoyed by us. "In the opening of the film," Hitchcock continues, "we show how he treats birds, animals. He thinks they should be in nice cages, and very happy, and so forth."

Hitchcock is inviting us to understand the cages in the film's first scene as symbolic of modern man's relationship to nature. They represent "enframing": nature is commodified, "turned into products for use and enjoyment." In the bird shop, Mitch asks Melanie, "Doesn't this make you feel awful? . . . All these innocent little creatures caged up like this?" Melanie speaks for modern man when she responds, cluelessly, "Well, we can't just let them fly around the shop, you know." It is as if she were unable to conceive of the birds as anything other than property. When Mitch playfully asks Melanie if he can "see" one of the canaries, he holds out his hand, as if "seeing" the bird means grasping it. (Though I should acknowledge that he does this to trick Melanie into letting one of the canaries out of its

9 Rare 1963 *The Birds* Interviews with Alfred Hitchcock & Tippi Hedren, https://www.youtube.com.

cage.) Here I cannot resist mentioning that Alan Watts translated the Taoist term *wu wei* (a concept not unlike Heidegger's *Gelassenheit*, to which I will turn in the next chapter) as literally meaning "don't grasp the bird."

Hitchcock continues: "Now, the film shows that man takes nature for granted. But if it turns on him, then he's in trouble." This and Hitchcock's earlier statement that "man must be responsible to nature" risk creating the impression that some kind of banal "environmentalist" or "conservationist" message is intended here. But there is something much deeper going on. He illustrates the point about nature "turning on" man with the following example: "He digs uranium out of the ground, and look at the trouble he's in from that."

In other words, it is not just a matter of "taking care" of nature; we must also recognize that nature is not merely a passively yielding commodity for our enjoyment and manipulation. Recall his comment that man "cannot assume that nature is always [beneficent]." Modern man deludes himself in thinking that he knows nature and can control it. In fact, it contains mystery—a dark mystery that we delve into at our peril. Our insistence on trying to make nature fully transparent, our relentless, "Oedipal" pursuit of knowledge can have terrible consequences (Hitchcock alludes to the atomic bomb) and nature can "turn on us."

In the Bogdanovitch interview, Hitchcock states that the theme of *The Birds*, "generally speaking," is that "people are too complacent. [Melanie] represents complacency. But I believe that when people rise to the occasion, when catastrophe comes, they are all right." This comment seems to restrict the theme of complacency to the private lives of the characters (e.g., Melanie's aimless life of hobbies and practical jokes). But the interview I have been citing for the last several paragraphs confirms that the film deals with complacency on a deeper level.

Hitchcock states, "There's a general theme [in *The*

Birds] that in respect of man's, shall we say, taking nature for granted, it makes him complacent. He thinks he's the master of everything." The deeper "complacency" treated here is thus the modern, human pretension to mastery and control of nature. To be sure, these two "complacencies" intersect in the film, and this is one of the elements that gives *The Birds* such great power: it is when the human complacency about nature is shattered that the characters in the film overcome the complacency that marks their own individual lives (more on that in the next chapter).

Hitchcock's remarks continue as follows: "But if a man [is] in a thunderstorm, if he's afraid at all, or you see a woman in a thunderstorm, she immediately goes under the table in fear. Nature is there in its most fiercest [sic]. I don't think they've ever been able to make an atom bomb with anything like the power of a thunderstorm." We may want to quibble with this last point, but Hitchcock is really saying that, ultimately, nature's power is greater than man's; that all pretensions to be "master of everything" are shattered when we go under the table in fear, cowering from a storm.

Despite all our modern boasting, an instinctive fear of the power of nature is felt deep in our bones—and perhaps that is just why we boast. Essentially, it's the same reason we whistle when we walk past a graveyard in the dead of night. We *know*—deep down, deeper than any of Mrs. Bundy's knowledge—that nature can swat us whenever she wants to, and that she will never, ever give up all her secrets. It is certainly true, on one level, to say that *The Birds* is about our taking nature "for granted," and then learning that it contains depths and powers that dwarf us. On a more fundamental level, however, I would suggest that this is a film about the "mystery of being."

Heidegger points out that there is a huge difference between the Greek *phusis* and its usual Latinized translation, "nature." The difference basically consists in the fact that "nature" has come to have the connotation of a *collection* of things that offer themselves to us to be gazed upon or made over in some fashion. In Hitchcock's words, this is "nature" as "the beautiful scenery, the sea and the sky, the trees, everything [man] enjoys." By contrast, the Greek *phusis* suggests a dynamic process. The word is derived from *phuein*, meaning "to generate or grow." Heidegger writes:

> Now what does the word *phusis* say? It says what emerges from itself (for example, the emergence, the blossoming, of a rose), the unfolding that opens itself up, the coming-into-appearance in such unfolding, and holding itself and persisting in appearance—in short, the emerging-abiding sway. . . . *Phusis* is the event of *standing forth*. Arising from the concealed and thus enabling the concealed to take its stand for the first time.[10]

Essentially, Heidegger identifies *phusis* with being. For the Greeks, "nature" is the very activity of the world around us continually emerging, unfolding, arising, unconcealing, appearing to us (to use Heidegger's descriptors). Note, however, that there is a "*to us.*" Things only appear to a subject. They are only "unconcealed" to a subject from whom something can be hidden. They only "emerge" to a subject that stands outside them, experiencing their emergence from hiddenness. Thus, for *phusis*/being to "happen," the clearing is necessary. In other words, we must possess the fundamental "openness" spoken of earlier.

---

[10] Martin Heidegger, *Introduction to Metaphysics*, trans. Gregory Fried and Richard Polt (New Haven: Yale University Press, 2000), 15–16.

For us, things emerge from hiddenness into the clearing. But the hiddenness of things is never completely overcome. For every disclosure, there is a correlative hiddenness or closure. To take an extremely simple example, if I am looking at the top of the cigarette lighter, the bottom is concealed from me. If the front of the scarecrow is present to me, the back is absent. If I move around to the back, it is now present to me, and the front is absent. It is the same way in *all* instances of "seeing" or "knowing" beings: something is revealed, while simultaneously something else is held back and concealed.

Heidegger made much of Heraclitus's claim that "nature [*phusis*] loves to hide." There is an intrinsic and ineliminable mystery to being. Whatever we uncover, there is always something that remains covered. What characterizes modernity, and is at the very root of *das Gestell*, is the hubristic idea that this mystery, this absence, can be (or eventually will be) completely overcome, and all will become transparent to us, all will be known. And if all is knowable, then all is, in principle, manipulable. This is modernity's *will to power*.

Of course, this is disastrous foolishness, because the mystery, the concealing or "holding back" of being *cannot* be overcome. Further, not even our own being can be made fully transparent. In fact, it may be our own being that remains most mysterious of all. This is certainly what Heidegger thought. As I explained in the last chapter, Heidegger held that human beings are fated to try to make sense out of things, to bring things into the clearing. As a species, this is *what we do*—it is our essential being. Yet exactly *why* this is and *why* we make sense of things in the way we do, in any given epoch of being, remains a mystery to us.

The clearing is the ultimate condition that makes things knowable or intelligible to us. Given this, the clearing itself is *not* fully knowable or intelligible. The clearing hides as well. Indeed, Heidegger refers to the hiddenness of the clearing as *das Geheimnis*, the mystery. He speaks of *das Geheimnis des Daseins* (the mystery of ex-istence; i.e., of human being), and of *das vergessene Geheimnis des Daseins* (the forgotten mystery of ex-istence, especially forgotten by us moderns, who think all mystery has been cancelled).

In *The Birds*, we are brought face to face with the un-fathomable mystery of being: the being of nature, our own being, and the being of being itself. A new epoch of being, a new Event emerges and cancels the old epoch of "en-framing," of taking nature as fully transparent and manip-ulable. Nature arises, emerges, reveals itself in a new and terrifying way. But this revealing is simultaneously a con-cealing: the "new" nature, the nature we had never known before, is mysterious and inexplicable. And why this Event has occurred defies our reason. Echoing Mrs. Bundy, birds have indeed been on this planet since archaeopteryx, a hundred and twenty million years ago. Why did they wait all this time to start a "war against humanity"? Why now? What has changed?

The film, as everyone knows, provides no answers to these questions. In a chilling passage from the short story, du Maurier writes, "Nat listened to the tearing sound of splintering wood, and wondered how many million years of memory were stored in those little brains, behind the stabbing beaks, the piercing eyes, now giving them this instinct to destroy mankind with all the deft precision of machines."[11]

Those piercing eyes are bottomless pits. We can peer into them all we like, but nothing remotely human peers back. Only the abyss of dark, merciless, pre-human eons stares back at us, like the empty, black eye sockets of Dan Fawcett. Given another million years, we will still not un-

---

[11] Du Maurier, *The Birds*, 38.

derstand *anything*—anything at all about the abyss of nature and time. From where did it all come? Why this? Why now does it change? Where is it going? Where are we going? No answer.

In chapter two, I discussed the importance of *silence* in *The Birds*. It is used to create suspense, and to suggest the presence of the uncanny. A heavy silence pervades the film, and it is out of this silence that the bird attacks come. The birds usually appear out of nowhere, attack, and then disappear again. This conveys, in a visual and auditory manner, the dynamic of the clearing. The clearing is an absence, a "space" in which things emerge from hiddenness and reveal something of what they are, before retreating again into hiddenness. Silence is an absence as well.

Hitchcock's insistence on silence, and refusal to use a music score, even in the film's earlier, lighter scenes, creates a sense of ominousness and expectance. We have the sense that something new and quite possibly terrible is about to emerge from this silence. We wait for it, in the suspense created by "the master," and we are also thrown back on ourselves. Why does this silence affect me so? Why does it make me so uncomfortable? Why does it make me silent in response? Why does it make me wait? We are confronted, in other words, with the mystery of our own openness, and our own angst in the face of the ultimate unintelligibility of existence, which we normally suppress through such devices as laughter, idle chatter, gay music, busyness, and, indeed, going to the movies.

The silence of the film does indeed create a sense of the uncanny. In chapter two, I argued that the uncanny is the encounter with something hidden that now shows itself but *nonetheless remains hidden*. In other words, to be in the presence of the uncanny is to be confronted with a phenomenon that remains intransigently unintelligible. The uncanny is a form in which we encounter the mystery of being, and of our own openness to being.

Heidegger treats the idea of the uncanny in his famous discussion of "anxiety" (*Angst*) in *Being and Time*:

> *That about which one has anxiety is being-in-the-world.* . . . In anxiety, the things at hand in the surrounding world sink away, and so do innerworldly beings in general. . . . Anxiety . . . fetches Dasein back out of its entangled absorption in "the world." Everyday familiarity collapses. Dasein is individualized, but *as* being-in-the-world. Being-in enters the existential "mode" of *not-being-at-home*. The talk about "uncanniness" [*Unheimlichkeit*] means nothing other than this.[12]

In the next chapter, we will rejoin our protagonists, as they continue their struggle against the birds.

---

[12] Martin Heidegger, *Being and Time*, trans. Joan Stambaugh (Albany: State University of New York Press, 2010), 182–83.

CHAPTER SIX

Thinking out loud, Mitch begins to lay out an idea that would involve blanketing the town in smoke to drive away the birds. But just then, Melanie interrupts him. "Look!" she cries, pointing out the window. Whereas the skies had been free of birds a moment before, several gulls have swooped in and are flying low, shrieking angrily. Across the street, a gas station attendant is in the process of filling up a parked car. A gull dive bombs the man, striking him in the head. He spins backward, hitting the pavement and is knocked unconscious. The gasoline hose drops from the man's hand, fuel gushing from the nozzle and over the concrete.

"They're attacking again!" Mitch cries and, after ordering Melanie to stay in the restaurant, he rushes outside to help. Just as Mitch leaves, the frightened mother we met earlier comes running back into the restaurant, pulling her two children along with her. Melanie and several of the others watch at the window as Mitch examines the unconscious gas station attendant. But no one is paying any attention to the river of gasoline rushing across the pavement. Melanie watches as the gas flows under several parked cars. Then we see the salesmen we met earlier, about to climb into his car. He has an unlit cigar in his mouth and is fumbling for a match, oblivious to the fact that the gasoline is now pooling at his feet.

"Look at the gas! That man's lighting a cigar," Melanie says, her voice muffled, as Hitchcock shoots the group from behind the glass. They manage to get the window open and begin yelling at the salesman. "Get out of there! Don't drop that match! Mister, run!" they scream frantically. But it is no use. Just as he seems to hear them, the lit match begins burning his hand. Instinctively, he tosses it to the ground, shaking his singed fingers. The gas immediately ignites, and the man is consumed in flames. This, of course, sparks a chain reaction, as the long stream of gasoline covering the parking lot ignites. Hitchcock intercuts the ignition of this gas, as it reaches the filling station and explodes, with four reaction shots from Tippi Hedren as she follows the progress of the flames. These are filmed in closeup. In these shots (taken, as usual, in soft focus) Hedren is absolutely motionless, her face frozen in horror, as the actors behind her continue to move normally. The effect is highly stylized, and, once more, Hedren exudes a kind of unearthly loveliness. This sequence is yet another illustration of Hitchcock prioritizing beauty and arresting images over realism.

At this point, the director unexpectedly removes us from the midst of this chaos and places us in the air, high above Bodega Bay. We see the town from above, but from no particular point of view. The shot is clearly not taken from a high building, as there are no tall buildings in Bodega Bay, nor is it taken from an aircraft, as the camera is motionless. In fact, like so much else in *The Birds*, this is a trick composite shot. Albert Whitlock created a matte painting showing a fictionalized representation of Bodega Bay. Back at Universal Studios, a fire was started in a parking lot with men running around it, representing what see from ground level in the film, and this was photographed through the glass matte painting, from a hillside. None of this footage, in short, is actually of Bodega Bay.

Hitchcock holds this shot, and all we hear is the low rushing of wind, and the very faint cries of the men below. After seven seconds, a gull appears on the righthand side of the screen—then another and another, until the screen is filled with angry, cawing gulls, all headed for the town below. These gulls were shot separately and then rotoscoped one by one into the footage utilizing Whitlock's matte work (a process that took technicians three months). Once again, the sounds made by the birds here, which are genuinely frightening, were produced electronically by the team of Remi Gassmann and Oskar Sala. While we completely accept these as sounds made by the birds, it is interesting to note that they do not sound like actual seagulls.

It would be interesting to make a careful comparison of the actual sounds of the birds depicted in the film with the effects contributed by Gassmann and Sala. My suspicion is that there would be significant disparities. Subliminally, we register them as what they are: false and artificial. This helps to negate the familiarity of the birds in the film, and to portray them as strange and uncanny. Over the course of the film, these effects become increasingly unrealistic, until by the time we reach the climactic siege on the Brenner house, they sound like avant-garde electronic music.

The shot of Bodega Bay seen from the air, with gulls massing for attack, lasts a little more than twenty seconds. Critics have usually taken it to be a "birds-eye view." In other words, Hitchcock seems here to remove us from the human perspective and to show the action from the point of view of the birds—from the inhuman point of view. Production designer Robert Boyle has disputed this, however:

> Hitchcock likes to put actors into situations he identifies with. He himself suffers from acrophobia, so he takes the audience high above the town in a "balloon" shot, which he called "God's point of view." Many people thought that it was supposed to represent a bird's eye view, but it was not intended to be from any particular point of view. It was supposed to take you away from all the confusion below and re-establish the audience.

One factor that supports Boyle's position is that the camera is not in motion: if it were the perspective of a bird would it not be in motion? I would argue, however, that things are somewhat more complicated than this.

First of all, it is perfectly natural for audiences to take this shot as the "birds' eye view," and Hitchcock is pretty much inviting us to do this. More importantly, however, whether this is a "birds' eye view" or a "God's eye view" it *actually comes to the same thing*, because the point of view is *inhuman*. The reason the shot is so disturbing is that it is threatening: the human becomes small and vulnerable, seen from the perspective of something that looms over it, ready to engulf it. The shot reinforces the "apocalyptic" tone that has already been established by the dialogue in the Tides. *Something* (the great unknown) is emerging from the heavens to threaten humanity. The "something" is seagulls—but then again it is not. It is the familiar now made frighteningly unfamiliar; it is the uncanny.

There is now general panic in Bodega Bay as hundreds of seagulls begin targeting every exposed human being in the vicinity of the pier. Cast and crew have reported that of all the birds, the seagulls were the most unpredictable and vicious, and would deliberately try and attack their eyes. Melanie and some of the Tides' patrons and employees make for the door, but quickly flee back into the restaurant when they see the carnage unfolding around them—all except Melanie, that is. She should have joined the others, but instead she foolishly seeks refuge inside a nearby telephone booth. This is, of course, an opportunity to set up some new frights for the audience, via a series of brilliant camera angles. It is one of the most famous sequences in the film, and in any of Hitchcock's work. Above all, it is a triumph of editing.

Melanie shuts herself in the glass phone booth, which affords her (and us) a panoramic view of the chaos that ensues. Hitchcock shoots Hedren from multiple angles, including from directly above. Recall Mitch's line early on in the film: "Back in your gilded cage, Melanie Daniels." The phone booth is not exactly gilded, but the symbolism is obvious: it is Melanie, and man, that are now caged. Gulls seem to deliberately target her, and it proves impossible for her to leave the phone booth. She attempts to open the door, but immediately a gull tries to enter, and Melanie has to push it away. At one point a horse drawn wagon comes careening into view and overturns, its driver nowhere to be seen. The horses have been panicked by the gulls. A man stumbles by the booth being attacked by gulls, his face streaked with blood. Though he says nothing, he seems to be pleading for help, but Melanie simply stares at him in horror. (This part of the sequence, unfortunately, comes across as somewhat hokey, largely due to the uncredited actor's melodramatic expression.)

As with many scenes in the film, the footage is enhanced by special effects. Some of the birds are rotoscoped into images of the town, and fake prop birds are used in several shots (the bird that attempts to enter the booth is very obviously fake). Just as in the scene where the schoolchildren are attacked by crows, the editing ensures that our eye never lingers on anything long enough to fully register the fakery. (At least this was the idea; the result is less successful with today's audiences, who are much more accustomed to processing rapidly changing images.) I have already noted that personnel from several film studios collaborated on the special effects for *The Birds*, notably Ub Iwerks of Disney. For this scene, Hitchcock utilized the services of MGM's Bob Hoag, who needed a team of thirty technicians to complete work on just this one sequence, which lasts less than a minute and a half. When it came time to edit the scene, Hitchcock requested that any footage of Hedren standing still be eliminated: he wanted her to be seen as constantly in motion.

The climax of the sequence is thrilling: in rapid succession, two gulls hurl themselves, kamikaze-like, against the booth, shattering the glass. The effect is completely convincing, and Hedren looks like she is in real danger from the flying glass. (She may well have been!) Indeed, despite my minor quibbling, the entire sequence is very effective, and contains some of the best special effects work in the film.

Finally, Mitch comes to rescue Melanie, pulling her out of the phone booth and back into the restaurant. The interior of the Tides is eerily quiet, and at first the restaurant seems deserted. We can hear the screeching of the gulls outside, but after a while that noise fades as well. Once more, the birds mysteriously end their attack and disappear. Mitch and Melanie scan the restaurant for signs of life, and then discover that the women are huddled in the short hallway leading to the restrooms. Fourteen or fifteen women are gathered there, plus the two children seen earlier, their terrified mother clutching them. The women's faces convey fear, but also defeat. One of them, an older woman with a green scarf tied around her head, has a face like an abused Basset Hound. Curiously, however, some of them bear another expression: some seem to be glaring at Mitch and Melanie. Or is it just Melanie?

This scene contains one of the most significant moments in the entire film—but if you blink, you will miss it. Seated in the hallway is Mrs. Bundy. Hitchcock has all the other women face the camera—except Ethel Griffies, who has her back to us. She is also the only woman (initially) who is shown alone in a close up. And she is trembling. The shot lasts barely two seconds. Hitchcock does not hit us over the head with it, but the point is crystal clear. Mrs. Bundy represents the hubris of modern man, who thinks he has laid bare nature's secrets and made her predictable and manipulable. Well, the hubris has now been knocked out of this old bag. She knows now that she knows nothing, so she sits trembling before the Unknown God.

Evan Hunter's "final draft" of the screenplay—dated March 2, 1962, just days before photography began—contains some surprises for those who remember this scene in the restaurant. To begin with, Mrs. Bundy is not described as trembling—far from it. In the script, the terrified mother says "Why are they doing it?! Why are they doing it . . . ?!" This is then followed by an indication that Mrs. Bundy will respond. However, instead of an actual line from Mrs. Bundy, Hunter inserts a notation in parentheses and square brackets that reads as follows: "([Mrs. Bundy offers a weak explanation of why the birds could have gone berserk like this. This information should be obtained from Dr. Stager.])" "Dr. Stager" refers to Kenneth Stager, an ornithologist at the Natural History Museum of Los Angeles County, who advised Hitchcock and Hunter on the film.

So, as originally planned, Mrs. Bundy was not to be seen as chastened at all. Instead, she would still have been prating. But Hitchcock clearly wanted to say something different here, and so the idea of Mrs. Bundy making another speech was dropped. Instead of a speech, she is rendered speechless. (Just as Lydia, instead of screaming when she finds Dan Fawcett's body, which Hunter's script had specified, instead is unable to scream.) In the finished film, this moment with Mrs. Bundy is followed by important (and very memorable) dialogue that also does not figure in Hunter's late draft of the screenplay. The terrified mother (whose name is never revealed) asks "Why are they doing this?! Why are they doing this?!"—just as in Hunter's script (though *it* was changed to *this*). She then rises from her seat and starts directly toward the camera, which represents Melanie's point of view.

"They said when you got here the whole thing started," she stammers. So now we know why Melanie has been getting these looks: they have been talking about her in her absence. In the space of about five minutes of screen time, these "modern" women have completely abandoned reason and have reverted to superstition. Burn the witch! Hitchcock intercuts the crazed woman with reaction shots from Melanie, who just looks baffled. "Who are you?" demands the woman, becoming increasingly hysterical. "*What* are you? Where did you come from?" As she approaches closer and closer to the camera, we see that Hitchcock has lit the woman's eyes to make her seem mad.

"I think you're the cause of all this," she says, now in tight closeup. "I think you're evil! Evil!!" she shrieks—and Melanie slaps her. Or, rather, the slap is suggested by a shot of Hedren swinging her arm, plus a reaction shot of the woman clasping her hands to her face (looking uncannily like the figure in Munch's *The Scream*), plus a sound effect. Surprised by her own reaction, Melanie collapses into Mitch's arms. The woman immediately seems to come to her senses, as if the slap has broken some kind of spell. The actress who plays her, Doreen Lang, is convincingly unhinged in this scene. For these few seconds of hysteria, her name in the opening credits appears set off and in larger type on the card that features the minor players.

It is quite interesting that this dialogue was inserted into the script so late in the process of planning the film. It certainly provides a dramatic climax to the entire sequence involving the restaurant, and the attack on the town. But is that the reason it is there? First, let us note that the woman succeeds in planting an idea in the audience's mind. The bird attacks do indeed begin with Melanie's arrival in Bodega Bay. In fact, the first attack is on Melanie (the gull hitting her while she is in the motorboat). The second "attack" is the gull hitting Annie's door, while Melanie is staying with Annie, and just after Melanie has promised Mitch that she will attend Cathy's party. It seems we are being invited to ask if all of this might somehow be about Melanie.

However, this could simply be a red herring. After all, Melanie was nowhere near the Fawcett farm when Dan's eyes were pecked out. Hunter's original ending to the film was completely abandoned by Hitchcock and never shot. It involved Melanie and the Brenners driving through Bodega Bay and out of the town. Along the way, they see the devastation wrought by the birds, including dead bodies. Years later, Hunter (who was generally dissatisfied with Hitchcock's treatment of his script) said this:

> The Hitchcock ending conveyed the impression . . . that what happened . . . may have been an isolated experience brought on by God knows what— Melanie's flighty earlier days? Lydia's rejection of her? Who knows? By extending the screenplay to show havoc wreaked in town, we dismiss any possibility of this having been a personal bird vendetta against a small group of people.[1]

In short, Hunter wanted to deliberately *exclude* the possibility that Melanie (or anyone else) is the focus of the attacks. However, by eliminating Hunter's ending, and insisting on the addition of the crazed woman's accusations against Melanie, Hitchcock has signaled that he *wants* the audience to consider this as a possibility. In general, Hunter's criticisms of the film indicate that he favored a more literal approach: he wanted a clearer indication of why the birds are attacking—hence the many hints in his original screenplay—and he objected to the "indefinite" ending Hitchcock imposed on the film.

---

[1] Kyle B. Counts and Steve Rubin, "The Making of Alfred Hitchcock's *The Birds*," *Cinemafantastique*, vol. 10, no. 2. (Fall 1980).

Hunter has also been extremely dismissive of the idea that there is any psychological or philosophical depth to the film. He later said, "I think Hitch is putting the world on when he pretends there is anything meaningful about *The Birds*. We were trying to scare the hell out of people. Period."

Well, that may have been what *he* was trying to do, but the changes Hitchcock makes to the script indicate that the director had his own agenda (though he definitely wanted to frighten the audience as well!). Summing up, let's consider some of Hitchcock's changes to the script:

1. The elimination of all explanations, no matter how flimsy, for why the birds attack. This includes Melanie's tongue-in-cheek "Marxist" theory of the bird revolution (in the deleted scene), and the hypothetical speech by Mrs. Bundy explaining the bird attacks.

2. The insertion of the crazed woman's accusations against Melanie.

3. The insertion of a shot showing Mrs. Bundy trembling—her self-satisfied scientism having been refuted.

4. The insertion of dialogue concerning Melanie's relationship to her mother, who abandoned her when she was small. (This creates a psychological sub-plot or sub-theme, which achieves resolution in the final scene.)

5. The elimination of Hunter's original ending, showing the escape of Melanie and the Brenners, and the insistence on an ambiguous ending.

All of this points to the obvious conclusion that Hitchcock was not just trying to scare the audience, but also trying *to make them think*. Hunter's script is quite literate (and I believe it contains more depth than he was aware of), but he was primarily a crime writer. Under the pen name "Ed McBain," Hunter (whose real name was Salvatore Albert Lombino) wrote fifty-five novels in the "87th Precinct" series between 1956 and his death in 2005. These were police procedural thrillers that aimed purely at telling a good mystery story. Hunter was a fine writer, but he was uninterested in "depth." It is clear from Hitchcock's changes to Hunter's work that he had larger ambitions.

In any case, while it is possible that Hitchcock may be creating a red herring by planting the idea in our minds that somehow the attacks are about Melanie, it is nonetheless an idea that we should seriously entertain. I will return to it in the next chapter. For now, let us take a closer look at the crazed woman's speech. As I have mentioned, she delivers her lines directly to camera, which represents Melanie's point of view. Of course, it is also *our* point of view: she looks directly at us and speaks to us. With this idea in mind—that she is speaking to us—let us consider her lines once more.

"They said when you got here the whole thing started." Indeed. It all started with Pandora, when she arrived with that damned box. Pandora was intended by Zeus as a bride for Prometheus ("fore thinker"), who stole fire from the gods and gave it to man. Smelling a trap, Prometheus handed her off to his brother Epimetheus ("after thinker"), and the rest is prehistory. Women are trouble. Has Melanie brought a box of tricks to Bodega Bay? Again, I'll return to the issue of whether Melanie is really the "focus."

"Who are you? *What* are you? Where did you come from?" We've been asking ourselves these questions for thousands of years, haven't we? And still, we don't know. Heidegger and the "Existentialism" he inspired (which, in important ways, distorted his ideas) speak of how human beings are "thrown" into this world and condemned to try to figure themselves out. Let's return for a moment to the story of Prometheus, specifically the "prequel" to his theft of fire. This part of the story is eloquently told by Bernard Stiegler in the 2004 documentary *The Ister*, which concerns Heidegger's ideas on technology:

> One day Zeus said to Prometheus, "the time has come for you, for us gods, to bring into the day the non-immortals." The non-immortals being animals and men. Prometheus, who is put in charge of this task, has a twin brother named Epimetheus. Epimetheus resembles Prometheus; he is his double. But in fact Epimetheus is his brother's opposite. Epimetheus is the god of the fault of forgetting. Prometheus is a figure of knowledge, of absolute mastery, total memory. Prometheus forgets nothing, Epimetheus forgets everything. Epimetheus says to his brother: "Zeus has given you this task—I want to do it! Me, me, me! I'll take care of it." Epimetheus is a rather simple-minded brother, and Prometheus is fond of him. He dares not refuse and says, "Okay, you take care of it." So Epimetheus distributes the qualities. He will give the gazelle its speed, for example [and so on] . . . Now, as Epimetheus is distributing the qualities, he suddenly notices something . . . "There are no qualities left! I forgot to save a quality for man! . . . I still have to bring mankind, mortals, into the day." . . . But there are no qualities left to give him a form. So Prometheus goes to the workshop of the god Hephaestus, to steal fire.[2]

Stiegler takes fire to represent "technics" (i.e, that which issues from *technē*, including technology). This interpretation (which is not original with Stiegler) is not un-

---

[2] *Der Ister* (2004), directed by David Barison and Daniel Ross.

reasonable, since fire is used in cooking and making. But fire also is a means to dispel the natural darkness imposed on man by night or enclosed places; it is a tool man uses to bring things into the light. Thus, it also represents intellect. (Indeed, there is no reason to suppose that fire cannot represent both intellect and "technics," since, of course, they are intimately related.) For Heidegger, man is "thrown" into this baffling world and "condemned" to try and make it intelligible. His most fundamental intellectual task is to answer the crazed woman's questions: Who are you? What are you? Where did you come from? These are the fundamental questions of philosophy.

Hitchcock is inviting us to ask ourselves these questions, inviting us to see that we do not know the answers to them. *The Birds* shatters our self-confidence, our hubris, as I have argued already. It invites us to see that we have been asleep, dreaming in a world of "buildings and concrete" (to use Melanie's words in the deleted scene); a human-built world surrounded by a nature we thought we understood and had tamed. The crazed woman's questions awaken us from our slumbers, and we are reminded, momentarily, that not only is nature a mystery to us, *we do not even know ourselves*.

"I think you're the cause of all this," she says, and then shrieks, "I think you're evil! Evil!" To address this particular point, we have to look beyond the Greek mythological tradition to the biblical. Melanie may be Pandora, or she may be Eve. It was the woman who tempted the man to eat from "the tree of the knowledge of good and evil," and who thus brought about the fall, and stained man with original sin. Some Hebrew scholars believe that the "good and evil" referred to in the name of the tree is a literary device implying "everything." So that "knowledge of good and evil" implies a synoptic or complete knowledge of all things. When we say that we "searched high and low" we don't mean that we searched only two points; we mean that we searched *everywhere*. Similarly, knowledge of what is good and knowledge of what is evil would be knowledge of *all*, since these appear to exhaust the possibilities. If this interpretation is correct, then eating of the tree represents the acquisition of the power to make all things intelligible. This "opens the eyes" of Adam and Eve. They now see that they are naked—in other words, they behold things as they really are.

But this all comes at a price: expulsion from the garden, pain, and toil. To top it off, the serpent lied when he said that they would become "as gods"—just as God lied when he said that they would die if they ate of the tree. The fruit didn't go down well. Our eyes were opened, but a new blindness beset us: the inability to see the limits of our knowledge, and of our power to change nature. Does this make man evil?

For Hitchcock, a Catholic to the end, a believer in original sin, it certainly did. (Priests performed Mass in Hitchcock's home on the night he lay dying, in April 1980, and heard his confession.) Heidegger too was a Catholic, and we see the influence of the doctrine of original sin reflected in the Heideggerian-Sartrean language of man as "condemned" to make things meaningful, and to be free (it comes to the same thing).

Each of the characters we meet in this pivotal scene in the Tides Restaurant is really a human "type." Mrs. Bundy represents the hubris of man the "rational animal" who thinks he has laid bare the secrets of nature ("I *do* know," she says). Then there is the Cassandra, the soothsaying Celt at the end of the bar, drunk on beer and religion. There is the hysterical mother, who transforms into a torch-wielding, angry villager before our very eyes. There is the hardheaded and hard drinking "practical" businessman who thinks nature is there to be bulldozed ("get yourselves guns and wipe [the birds] off the face of the earth . . . Get rid of them. Messy animals."). There is the cowardly and dithering Sebastian Sholes, who'd rather somebody else dealt with this problem. We may not be "evil," but we certainly are a motley crew.

With the gulls now retreating, Mitch and Melanie leave the restaurant and make their way up the hill to Annie's house to retrieve Cathy. All is deathly quiet. As they approach the schoolhouse, they see that the crows are back and perched all over the building and on the playground. "Look, the crows again!" Melanie says breathlessly. But as they approach the little house with its picket fence, a still more horrifying sight awaits them.

CHAPTER SEVEN

Annie lies dead on the gravel leading to the front steps. Her arms and legs are streaked with blood, her face turned away from us. Annie's feet rest on the steps, but her right foot is twisted toward her other leg— indecorously, painfully, rigidly. She looks like a marionette tossed aside by a bored child who's moved on to something new. The gate stands open, suggesting Annie had no time to close it. "Oh, no!" Mitch cries, grimacing. "Stay here," he says to Melanie, and then moves closer to examine the body. Melanie watches from the street. When she sees Annie's face, she screams. Just at that moment, Hitchcock shows us a closeup of the side of Suzanne Pleshette's head. But before we can make out any details, Rod Taylor's hand quickly moves into frame and pointedly conceals Pleshette's eyes.

Those viewing the film at home can, of course, freeze the frame just before Taylor's hand appears. If they do, they will see that while Pleshette's face is bloodied, her right eye is visible, and no special makeup has been applied to it. Nevertheless, the clear suggestion is that Annie has been blinded by the birds, just as Dan Fawcett was.[1]

---

[1] Although it is a very effective sequence, the scene is nevertheless an example of what was once a common feature of Hollywood films: the inexplicable death (something that often afflicted beautiful actresses). Albert Whitlock reported that he was on the set that day and could not understand how the birds had killed Annie. "I said to Hitch, 'Something's bothering me. What does Suzanne die of, because she only has a few scratches?'" Hitchcock replied with a twinkle, "Who knows?" See Moral, *The Making of Hitchcock's* The Birds, 123. Moral also reports that during the shooting of the death scene, one of the crows flew over Pleshette and pooped on her, causing the

Convulsed with horror, Melanie crosses her arms, hands clutching her shoulders, and doubles over. Then, in a childlike voice, she asks "Cathy? Where's Cathy?" Camille Paglia correctly notes that "she has begun to regress—a slide that will continue until film's end."[2] We have heard this childlike voice before: in the scene on the dunes, when Melanie spoke of how her mother abandoned her.

Cathy, face streaked with tears, is staring at them from one of the windows. She is safe, unharmed. Mitch enters through the front door and leads Cathy to the end of the porch, and down the side steps, to avoid his young sister having to encounter Annie's body. Then he lifts her up and over the fence, where she and Melanie embrace. Melanie asks Mitch not to leave Annie's body on the gravel. With eyes that convey great sadness, and possibly also regret, Mitch takes off his blazer and drapes it over his former love, then carries her body into the house. (He will spend the rest of the film in shirt sleeves.)

The trio quickly make for Melanie's car, which has been sitting by the school since Melanie arrived there some hours ago. As the crows begin to caw ominously, Mitch frantically closes the convertible's top and they all pile in. Mitch is in the driver's seat, despite the fact that it is Melanie's car. This is a small, but significant act of masculine assertion.

It is once the car gets underway that Cathy, who is still clinging to Melanie, collapses into hysterics. "On our way back from taking Michele home . . . we heard the explosion and went outside to see what it was," Cathy says, choking back tears. "All at once the birds were everywhere. All at once she pushed me inside . . . and they covered her! Annie! She pushed me inside!" She then begins

---

actress and everyone else present to convulse with laughter.

² Camille Paglia, *The Birds* (London: Bloomsbury—British Film Institute series, 2020), 81. (Originally published 1998.)

sobbing uncontrollably. It is a touching moment, very well played by young Veronica Cartwright.

What are we to make of this character, Annie Hayworth, and of her death? Dramatically, the death serves an obvious purpose. This is the first time a character we know and care for has been killed by the birds. There is a moment after finding Annie's body where Mitch picks up some stones from the ground and, his face contorted in hate, is about to toss them at the crows. Melanie dissuades him from this. The death of Annie does not so much cause us to hate the birds, as to fear them even more. We knew that the situation was serious, but now we realize it can claim *us*—as we had identified with Annie and sympathized with her. Her death causes us to fear for the other characters, especially Melanie. What is to be their fate?

There is a larger significance to Annie's death, however. First of all, it is clearly an act of self-sacrifice. When Annie and Cathy went outside, the birds descended on them. Annie's first thought was not for herself, but for Cathy, whom she pushes inside. But Annie is not able to follow the child into the house: "all at once . . . they covered her." Cathy realizes the self-sacrificial nature of Annie's act by affirming, twice, "she pushed me inside." This is significant because Annie is portrayed earlier as being self-pitying and self-absorbed, just like the other major characters (with the exception of Mitch, who is self-absorbed, but seemingly not self-pitying). Nonetheless, she is likeable. (Pleshette was an excellent choice for the role, and for television sitcoms, as she exudes a kind of tough warmth that's extremely appealing.)[3]

---

[3] Tony Lee Moral notes that Hitchcock later stated that Annie died "because of her sense of duty to the school." Hitchcock compared her to a character in his *The 39 Steps* who was "doomed by his sense of duty." See Moral, *The Making of Hitchcock's* The Birds, 123.

It is from here on in *The Birds* that we will begin to see some resolution to the problems of these characters. In previous chapters, we have seen that Hitchcock described them as exhibiting "complacency," especially Melanie. I have also argued that the film is a meditation on how modern complacency as such is destroyed through an encounter with the uncanny. But let us now ask *why* these characters in particular, and modern man generally, exhibit complacency. The answer has to do with *abandonment*, understood in both biographical and metaphysical senses.

Melanie was abandoned by her mother, literally. Without a positive female role model in her life, she seems to drift, seeking attention from all and sundry, jumping into fountains, playing practical jokes, and enjoying the role reversal of pursuing men (in a motorboat, no less).

The Brenner family was "abandoned" by Frank Brenner, Mitch's father, whose untimely death has thrown his family off-kilter. As Annie implies in conversation with Melanie, Lydia was devastated by Frank's death. As a result, she fears abandonment (as Annie literally puts the matter). In turn, this has caused her to cling to Mitch as if he were a surrogate husband, and to sabotage his relationships with women.

The result for Mitch is that he is caught in an Oedipal relationship with his mother and cannot grow as a man. In consequence, Annie was abandoned by Mitch and left to wither in spinsterhood across the bay.

In what sense is modern man "abandoned"? Abandoned by the gods, Heidegger would say. He speaks in more than one text of the "flight of the gods." In *Introduction to Metaphysics* he writes, "on the earth, all over it, a darkening of the world is happening. The essential happenings in this darkening are: the flight of the gods, the destruction of the earth, the reduction of human beings to a mass, the preeminence of the mediocre."[4] In later texts, the idea of the loss of the gods (*Entgötterung*) or their flight becomes more important. But what does it mean? Heidegger's idea of "the gods" is complex, and it is impossible to do justice to it here. At the risk of greatly oversimplifying things, the flight of the gods in modernity means the apparent loss of any dimension of meaning to things that does not reduce to utility.

In post-war modernity, all beings, including human beings, are reduced to the status of a "standing reserve" that is continually being consumed and replenished. All that exists is standardized, commodified, and interchangeable. The modern world is, in its essence, an engine of consumption whereby these beings are continually being used up and then replaced. Further, the modern world exists for no higher purpose other than this cycle of consumption and replacement. Abandoned to this fate, most fall into line and consume with, indeed, abandon. Even their self-conception is defined as "standing reserve" (i.e., they understand themselves merely as material for use: "consumers," "employees," etc.). To fill this empty void called modern "life," they busy themselves with consumption and with pointless and trivial distractions—just as Melanie Daniels does. And they wait to die—whereupon they will be replaced by equally replaceable consumers.

This lasts until there is a shift in the meaning or being of things—until another Event comes along (we discussed Heidegger's concept of *das Ereignis*, the Event, in chapter four). If it comes. I have argued in this series that *The Birds* represents the coming of such an Event; a sudden and fundamental shift in meaning. This is not something that can be brought about or controlled by human beings. It simply comes. (Though, to a very limited extent, human beings can prepare for it, or prepare the ground for it.)

---

[4] Martin Heidegger, *Introduction to Metaphysics*, 47.

There may not be a next Event, and if it arrives it may not "cancel" the modern understanding of beings as "standing reserve." It may usher in something worse (though that is hard to imagine). But let us suppose that it does indeed cancel modernity, and even that it heralds something of a return to attitudes and ways of being that have their roots in pre-modernity (as Hitchcock seems to suggest—e.g., with the townswomen's sudden return to "superstition"). Then such an Event would be our "salvation" in the sense that it might heal us of the abandonment I have spoken of. In *The Birds*, the characters are eventually healed of their own abandonment through their conflict with nature suddenly gone mad.

We will see how the other characters heal by the end of the film, but Annie is the first. As I have noted, she is healed through an act of self-sacrifice, which is yet another form of "abandonment," the abandonment of the ego and its pretensions, fixations, and self-pity. This idea of self-abandonment is, as it were, the "other end" of what Heidegger calls *Gelassenheit*. This term literally means "having-let-go-ness." The term originates with Meister Eckhart, and Eckhart commentators have sometimes glossed it as "serenity." Heidegger translators have rendered it "releasement," or even "letting-beings-be." All these translations make a certain amount of sense.

Thomas Sheehan explains *Gelassenheit*'s meaning as follows: "the point of . . . releasement (*Gelassenheit*) is to recognize the intrinsic hiddenness of one's appropriation, to *actively leave* it in its hiddenness, and to live, finitely and mortally, from out of it."[5] Recall that what Heidegger refers to as "the clearing" (*die Lichtung*) is the "space" opened up by Dasein, by human being, in which the being or meaning of things becomes present to us. For

---

[5] Sheehan, *Making Sense of Heidegger*, 257. Italics in original.

Heidegger, the clearing is intrinsically "hidden" because it is the condition that makes possible all intelligibility; thus, it cannot itself be made intelligible. The clearing and fundamental changes in the clearing (i.e., the Event, or what Sheehan calls "appropriation") remain mysteries to us.

This presents us with two choices. We could deny mystery outright and seek to cancel hiddenness; to demand that everything must become completely present to us. This is the way of the "Absolute Ego" of the German idealists (specifically J. G. Fichte and his followers) which seeks to cancel the otherness of the other; to overcome the subject-object distinction. It is also the way of modernity, which demands that everything be transparent and manipulable. It is also the way of nihilism, for such a demand literally destroys the world (from Latin dēstruō: dē-, as in "un-," + struō, "I build").

The other way is to surrender to mystery. This is *Gelassenheit*. But in order for this "releasement" to happen, there must be an abandonment of the ego's will to power.[6]

---

[6] This is something of a simplification of Heidegger's position. His real answer to the Fichtean-modern position is *not* to say something along the lines of "the subject must surrender to the otherness of the object." Rather, he wishes to critique the subject-object distinction *as such*. So long as we conceive of ourselves as "subjects" existing in separation from an "external world," within an "interior," then beings *must* present themselves as "others" pegged by the "subject" as "objects" of investigation or manipulation. To *demand* that we "let them be" is to imply that we could, if we wished, *not* let them be and truly make good on our will to make them fully transparent and manipulable. What must thus be overcome is the very idea of a subject existing "apart." This is a project that is already announced in *Being and Time* but is really only fully developed in Heidegger's late teaching of the "fourfold." Incidentally, the points just made also serve to identify the fallacy inherent in today's "environmentalism." Instead of challenging the idea of man as "master of nature," that movement implicitly affirms a

Certainly, Eckhart would have understood this, and I doubt Heidegger would have disputed it. By the end of *The Birds*, we will have been presented with a shocking symbolic enactment of self-abandonment/releasement, performed by Melanie Daniels.

To return to our story, Mitch, Melanie, and Cathy now go back to the Brenner home to prepare for the next battle in the "bird war." Of course, the smart thing would have been for them to have picked up Lydia and high-tailed it out of Bodega Bay, as far away as possible. But then we would have been deprived of the film's dramatic, final act.

It is now the early evening and Mitch is on a ladder, in the process of boarding up every window of the house. Melanie is helping by handing him wooden planks. Together, they look across the bay. Hitchcock shows us their point of view, which is another trick, composite shot. We see hundreds of black spots flying over the bay. Below them, white spots representing gulls speckle the surface of the water. The skies are grey and ominous. As noted in an earlier chapter, the skies over Bodega Bay were usually sunny during filming, so all the shots of overcast skies were matte paintings. An overhanging tree appears to have been painted in.

"It seems like a pattern, doesn't it?" says Mitch. "They strike and disappear, and then they start massing again. It doesn't look so very different, does it? A little smoke hanging over the town, but otherwise . . ." In the screenplay, but not in the finished film, Melanie says, "It does look very much the same, Mitch. This could be last week." To which Mitch replies, "It may not be last week again for a long, long time." In fact, it will never be last week again.

---

modern, Promethean conception of man as an omnipotent being capable of "destroying nature" if he wished, and if he does not mend his ways.

We learn that Melanie has been trying to call her father once more but that the phones are dead. Thankfully, the power is still on. Lydia calls to Mitch from inside the house, saying that she's hearing something on the radio. Mitch and Melanie rush inside, and then, with Lydia and Cathy, they stand anxiously in the living room, listening to the affected voice of the radio announcer:

> In Bodega Bay early this morning, a large flock of crows attacked a group of children who were leaving the school during a fire drill. One little girl was seriously injured and taken to the hospital in Santa Rosa, but the majority of children reached safety. We understand there was another attack on the town, but this information is rather sketchy. So far, no word has come through to show if there have been further attacks. [Then, the announcer's voice brightens:] On the national scene in Washington . . .

"Was that all?!" Mitch says with disgust, and then begins tending to the fire. Once more, these characters have been abandoned.

These scenes, and those to come, are loosely based on du Maurier's short story: just after boarding up the house, Nat and his wife listen to the radio hoping for some indication that help is on the way. In the short story as well, they are left with the impression that they have been abandoned; that no one takes their plight seriously. Unlike the film, they learn that strange bird activity has been reported all over the country. But the radio announcer almost seems to make light of the whole thing:

> Nat had the impression that this man, in particular, treated the whole business as he would an elaborate joke. There would be others like him, hundreds of them, who did not know what it was to struggle in

darkness with a flock of birds. There would be par-
ties tonight in London, like the ones they gave on
election nights. People standing about, shouting
and laughing, getting drunk. "Come and watch the
birds!"[7]

This observation is clearly a reflection of well-founded
class resentment: Nat is convinced that London elites do
not fundamentally care what happens to people in the
provinces. And he is correct. Just a few hours later, however, once the birds have created havoc for the country's
power centers, the quality of the radio announcer's voice
has changed: "His voice was solemn, grave. Quite different
from midday."[8]

In the film, this class dynamic is completely absent.
Melanie is a poor little rich girl. Though the Brenners have
a farm, they are not "farmers" in the sense in which Nat
and his family are. The Brenners are educated and upper
middle class. Mitch is an affluent criminal lawyer who
maintains an apartment in San Francisco. His father was
probably a successful businessman or quite possibly a
lawyer as well. Their living room is full of weighty tomes.[9]
Hunter's script specifies of Lydia that "There is nothing
agrarian-looking about her. She speaks with the quick
tempo of the city dweller, and there is lively inquiry in her
eyes."

The reason for this change is to provide the large, ur-
ban cinema audience with characters they can more easily
identify with. And, indeed, Hitchcock would have found it
hard to identify with real farmers. When rural America is

---

[7] Du Maurier, *The Birds*, 13.

[8] Du Maurier, *The Birds*, 23.

[9] There is a bit of a gaffe here, though: if one freezes the
frame and looks closely, one will see that the shelves sometimes contain multiple copies of the same exact book!

depicted in his films it is always a gentrified America with the feel of the English countryside, as in *The Trouble with Harry* and *Marnie*. About the closest you get to a real "salt of the earth" type in a Hitchcock film is the man Cary Grant meets at a crossroads in *North by Northwest*. But this change to the characters in *The Birds* also allows Hitchcock to make some interesting points he could not otherwise have made. As I have said repeatedly, the characters in the film are portraits of spoiled, complacent, self-absorbed modern people. This would have been impossible had the main characters remained simple rural types, since it is affluent urbanites who are the principal carriers of modern pathologies.

In the film, after hearing the brief news report about Bodega Bay, the radio continues to play in the background. Evan Hunter's script specifies what is heard, but in the finished film the radio plays at such a low volume under the dialogue it is impossible to tell whether the script is being followed to the letter. What Hunter had scripted, regardless of whether it was actually used, is worth taking a look at. From the news about Bodega Bay, the announcer segues into the latest news out of Washington, D.C. where the President has just given his State of the Union address to Congress. We then hear portions of the President's speech, addressing America's relations with the rest of the world:

> These various elements of our foreign policy lead as I have said to a single goal. The goal of a peaceful world of free and independent states. This is our guide for the present and our vision for the future— a free community of nations, independent but interdependent, uniting north and south, east and west, in one great family of man, outgrowing and transcending the hates and fears that rend our age. We will not reach that goal today or tomorrow. We

may not reach it in our lifetime. But the quest is the great adventure of our century. We sometimes chafe at the burdens of our obligations, the complexity of our decisions, the agony of our choices, but there is no comfort or security for us in evasion, no solution in abdication, no relief in irresponsibility . . .

And on and on. It is a series of empty political and moral platitudes—which is the whole point. Just as in du Maurier's story, while the platitudes fly fast and wet from establishment elites, our cast of characters fights for their lives against nature gone berserk. Previously, we thought we lived in a state of peaceful coexistence with the birds. Now they have turned into an implacable foe with whom it is impossible either to communicate or to reason. Was this hostility simmering beneath the surface the entire time? Are we ever really at peace with other species, or was Heraclitus right that all reality is actually a state of war? Meanwhile, the American President prates about the "family of man," and about "transcending hates and fears." The truth is that there is no "family of man," just like there is no "family of nature."

We are told in Isaiah 11:6-8 (the same book of the Bible quoted earlier by the drunk):

The wolf also shall dwell with the lamb, the leopard shall lie down with the young goat, the calf and the young lion and the fatling together; and a little child shall lead them. The cow and the bear shall graze; their young ones shall lie down together; and the lion shall eat straw like the ox. The nursing child shall play by the cobra's hole, and the weaned child shall put his hand in the viper's den.

But this is just bollocks. As Joseph Campbell said many

years ago, "No, the lion is going to eat the lamb, but that is the way of nature." Hates and fears will never be transcended; they are woven into the very fabric of existence. As we will see very soon, at least one of the characters in the film has drawn the correct *tribalist* conclusions from this.

It is after listening to the radio that Lydia begins showing definite signs of strain. She asks Mitch if he has made sure that the attic windows have been boarded up (they have). "When do you think they'll come?" she asks. Mitch replies that he doesn't know, and how could he? "If there are bigger birds, Mitch, they'll get into the house," she says, becoming increasingly agitated. "Maybe we ought to leave." Mitch rejects this suggestion, saying "Not now. Not while they're massing out there." "When?" Lydia asks crisply. "Where will we go?" She is now pointedly interrogating him.

Melanie and Cathy watch the scene unfold with evident concern. "What happens when we run out of wood?" Lydia demands. Exasperated, Mitch responds, "I don't know. We'll break up the furniture." It is at this point that Lydia explodes, screaming at him: "You don't know, you don't know! When will you know?! When we're all dead?! Like Annie?!" That last question is almost inaudible, as Cathy suddenly intervenes between the two of them and bursts into tears. To add insult to injury, Lydia adds, "If only your father were here . . . !"

Mitch is visibly wounded by this remark, and Lydia stops short, catching herself, realizing she has gone too far and said that which was supposed to remain unsaid. She has impugned his masculinity. Lydia has stunted her own son's growth as a man, emotionally blackmailing him into the role of surrogate husband, and undermining his relationships with women. But in the peculiar way of women, she is now mocking him for allowing her to do this; she is challenging him to stand up to her. Her reaction is not brought about by any specific failure in his recent actions. (How can he, in fact, know the answers to the questions with which she bombards him?) Rather, it is an expression of a general dissatisfaction with her son's unwillingness to challenge her, and to grow and become independent.

She had kept this hidden (and perhaps she was not consciously aware of it), but the crisis and her mounting anxiety have brought it into the open. There is dialogue in the original script which makes this whole unhealthy mother-son dynamic even more obvious, though it does not make it into the finished film. Originally, Mitch was to have responded to Lydia's outburst by saying, rather pathetically, "Mother! I'm trying my best!" Then, shaking his head, "I'm . . . trying . . . my . . ." This is Hunter trying to bring out more clearly the "predicament" of the Mitch character (which is not as clear in the finished film). Each of the characters is affected and transformed by their encounter with the birds. The effect on Mitch is to make him more of a man.

Hunter bemoaned the casting of Rod Taylor as Mitch, describing the actor as "so full of machismo you expect him to have a steer thrown over his shoulder."[10] A less overtly masculine actor might have brought out the character's weakness more clearly. Hitchcock stars James Stewart, Gregory Peck, or even Cary Grant (whose Roger Thornhill in *North by Northwest* is not unlike Mitch) could have pulled this off, but all were too old by this time to be romancing Tippi Hedren, and *far* too old to have an eleven-year-old sister.

It is possible to defend the casting of the hyper-masculine Taylor, on the grounds that even the most masculine *appearing* modern men are un-masculine in spirit.

---

[10] Counts and Rubin, "The Making of Alfred Hitchcock's *The Birds.*"

Putting it in the language of Julius Evola, the absence of "spiritual virility" is most striking when coupled with the presence of physical virility. The trouble is that this is lost on the audience, as the "developmental arc" of this character is the least clear in the entire film.

In any case, Lydia apologizes for her outburst, and it is quickly forgiven and forgotten. Mitch and Melanie step outside and look up at the darkening skies. Thousands of birds are flying overhead. "Where are they heading?" Melanie asks. Mitch suggests they are headed inland. "Santa Rosa?" Melanie asks. "Maybe," he says. This is the first suggestion that the "bird war" may be spreading to locations beyond Bodega Bay. There will be a further suggestion near the end of the film. In du Maurier's story, the attacks have spread across the entire UK. Hitchcock wanted to leave all of this indefinite, but, as I will suggest later, I think that the most likely outcome to the story is that the attacks do indeed spread far, far beyond Northern California.

We now dissolve to some point later in the evening, when the foursome is seated together in the living room, keeping vigil, waiting for the next onslaught. Coffee has been drunk. Lydia sits removed from the others in a chair between the piano and a wall. One of her hands grips the piano, the other is pressed against the wall. Her body language conveys extreme anxiety. Melanie and Cathy sit huddled together on the couch, holding hands. Melanie has one arm protectively around the girl's shoulder. Mitch is the only one who stands. He is checking and re-checking the fortifications he has created at the windows. A fire burns in the fireplace.

Suddenly, Cathy asks Mitch if she can bring the lovebirds into the room. "No!" shrieks Lydia. "But Mom," Cathy protests, "they're in a cage." "They're *birds*, aren't they?!" Lydia shoots back. Now, this is obviously not a "rational" response. Cathy is right: those little lovebirds will *not* be able to get out of their cage and do any mischief. But Lydia's response is not actually moved by such a concern. Instead, her tone and emphasis make clear that she speaks out of *hate*. It's "us vs. them" time. The birds are now, quite justifiably, the hated "other," the tribe at war with the humans.

Lydia's tribalism is a healthy, normal, and necessary response—and she is way ahead of the others. Women "get" these sorts of things on a deep, sub-rational level, no matter what duckspeak they've been taught to quack. Melanie gets that the crows were after the schoolchildren out of blind hate, for no reason other than to kill them (while the unfeminine Mrs. Bundy listens in disbelief). Annie gets what's coming when, at the children's birthday party, she says "that makes three times"—speaking, as Camille Paglia brilliantly observes, "like a Roman augur."[11] The women in the Tides get that something uncanny is happening, that all the jazz about "reason" is out, and that the new girl in town may somehow be responsible.

Humoring his mother, Mitch tells Cathy that the lovebirds should be left in the kitchen. Then he heads there himself, as Lydia scans the ceiling as if scanning the skies. In the kitchen, he examines the doors and windows to make sure they are securely covered. On his way out, Mitch looks down at the lovebirds, perched placidly in their cage, on a table by the door. There is a slight suggestion of hatred in his eyes as he looks at them. Then he rejoins the others. They all sit and wait.

Cathy suddenly asks Mitch, "Why are they doing this? The birds?" Mitch responds, "I don't know, honey." Cathy persists: "Why are they trying to kill people?" "I wish I could say," he answers. In the script, Mitch adds, "But if I could answer that, I could also tell you why people are trying to kill people." Thankfully, this line was eliminated

---

[11] Paglia, *The Birds*, 61.

before shooting.

Unable to sit still any longer, Lydia quietly rises and moves to the coffee table. Slowly but with evident tension, she begins gathering the coffee cups onto the tray, as Melanie watches her intently with sympathetic eyes. Lydia removes the tray to the kitchen and then returns. All of them keep their eyes on the ceiling, scanning it, listening. It is at this point that Cathy becomes literally sick with fear. Lydia starts to rise to go to her daughter, but Cathy seems to want Melanie's help. Together, they move off-screen, presumably to the bathroom, and we hear Cathy coughing as she vomits.

When Melanie and Cathy return, it begins.

CHAPTER EIGHT

At first, we hear the sound of birds singing. The sound is pretty and harmless. Is it the lovebirds in the kitchen? Then we hear fluttering and flapping. This grows louder and louder, and the pretty singing of a moment before is replaced by angry cawing and screeching. It is one of the most interesting scenes in the entire film. This is especially true if one watches it with the sound off. All the characters behave in ways that are completely understandable, but also completely irrational.

Lydia rises from her chair, clawing the wall next to her as if she is trying to climb it. Cathy leaves Melanie and rushes into her mother's arms. Then the two of them, in embrace, begin moving along the walls, from corner to corner within the room, in a futile attempt to seek shelter against a threat that is so far invisible. Hitchcock shoots Tippi Hedren from a low angle as she backs onto the sofa, terrified. Then she sits, as far back to the wall as she can possibly get, drawing her legs up onto the cushions. Her small hands clutch at the arm of the sofa and the wall behind her. Meanwhile, Mitch leaps into action, and begins madly throwing log after log onto the fire—determined to do something, anything.

I do, in fact, encourage readers to watch the scene a second time with the sound muted. Without the sound effects of the attacking birds, the behavior of the characters seems neurotic to the point of insanity, given that *nothing is there*. It is worthwhile quoting at length Hitchcock's remarks to Francois Truffaut about shooting this scene (which does not occur in Evan Hunter's screenplay):

> I can tell you the emotions I went through. I've always boasted that I never look at a script while I'm

shooting. I know the whole film by heart. I've always been afraid of improvising on the set because, although one might have the time to get a new idea, there isn't sufficient time in the studio to examine the value of such an idea. . . . But I was quite tense, and this is unusual for me because as a rule I have a lot of fun during the shooting. When I went home to my wife at night, I was still tense and upset. Something happened that was altogether new in my experience: I began to study the scenario as we went along, and I saw that there were weaknesses in it. This emotional siege I went through served to bring out an additional creative sense in me. I began to improvise. For instance, the whole scene of the outside attack on the house by birds that are not seen was done spontaneously, right on the set. I'd almost never done anything like that before, but I made up my mind and quickly designed the movements of the people inside the room. I decided that the mother and the little girl would dart around to search for shelter. There was no place to run for cover, so I made them move about in contradictory directions, a little like rats scurrying into corners. I deliberately shot Melanie Daniels from a distance because I wanted to make it clear that she was recoiling from nothing at all. What could she be drawing back from? She cringes back into the sofa and she doesn't even know what she's recoiling from.[1]

---

[1] Francois Truffaut, *Hitchcock* (New York: Simon & Schuster, 1983), 289–90.

Tony Lee Moral also quotes Hitchcock saying, in another source, "The girl retreats from nothing. So her image was emptiness in the foreground, symbolising nothing." See Moral, *The Making of Hitchcock's* The Birds, 133.

Since the actors needed something to react to, Hitchcock brought in a drummer. Tippi Hedren later recalled,

> When we arrived on the set we saw this drummer sitting there with a huge drum. We didn't know Hitch had planned this. In the scene, the tension is supposed to slowly build as the birds start to attack the house. Even Hitchcock, as fine a director as he is, couldn't get a bunch of birds to act that way, so he got the idea of using the drum roll to help us react and to build up the tension. For me, it was the most effective scene in the film.[2]

This reminds me of the sort of techniques that were used to elicit reactions from performers in silent films (and one of the keys to understanding Hitchcock is that he remained a silent film director throughout his entire career). Like the characters, the audience is forced to use its imagination—to try to visualize the attack.

The scene also fits in with the mood of "existential angst" I have argued (in previous chapters) pervades the entire film. Melanie is indeed, as Hitchcock says, "recoiling from nothing"—or is it from *the* nothing? Her world—in Heidegger's sense of "world"—has ended, and a new one is taking shape. This change is absolutely unintelligible. It comes from out of depths unfathomed by the human mind. Whither is it going? That too is a great, terrible blank. The mysterious change in the birds comes out of the abyss, and now our characters face a future which is also abyssal. What is to come, now that everything they thought they knew has been overturned? Who can say? And so they seal their house, turning it (ironically) into a cage, then climb the furniture and career around the

---

[2] Counts and Rubin, "The Making of Alfred Hitchcock's *The Birds*."

room, driven mad by fear of nothing.

But let us now consider the sound created for this sequence, for it is highly interesting in itself. From the beginning of the bird attack to the very end, not a line of dialogue is spoken by the actors. Instead, the audio is entirely focused upon the artificial bird sounds Sala and Gassmann created using the Trautonium. As the story progresses, these sound effects become more and more artificial—in other words, less and less like the sounds of actual birds. In this scene, the artificiality becomes so extreme that the soundtrack seems more like an avant-garde electronic music score.

There are moments where the effects are reminiscent of something created for *Doctor Who* by the BBC Radiophonic Workshop. This is especially the case in the two or three seconds preceding the moment when the first birds actually break through one of the windows. There is a high-pitched whirring, whizzing noise followed by a rushing sound—just before we hear breaking glass, as a gull penetrates one of the shutters Mitch thought he had securely closed. These electronic sounds depict nothing; in other words, they are not re-creations of any actual sounds made by birds. They are simply terrifying. The scene is so compelling that even on multiple viewings it does not occur to us that real birds *cannot* make these sounds!

As already mentioned, one gull and then another manages to get behind the shutter Mitch had closed over the living room window, and to break the glass. There follows a very realistic struggle, wherein Mitch pushes the birds out and tries to get the shutter closed again. There is one shot where we simply see Mitch's hand trying to grasp the knob on the shutter as his flesh is attacked by the gulls. In this shot, the hand does not belong to Rod Taylor but to Ray Berwick, the trainer of the birds. The blood here looks fake, but in fact it was entirely real, as the angry gulls mercilessly pecked their trainer's hand with their sharp beaks.

Mitch finally succeeds in fastening the shutter closed by tying the knob to the window using an electrical cord from a table lamp. Then he briefly tends to his mother, still clutching Cathy, who seems terrified to the point of madness. Melanie has meanwhile crawled up the sofa and has begun to slither, for lack of a better word, along the fireplace mantel. Unlike Lydia, however, she is not completely paralyzed with fear, and has the presence of mind to try to tend to Mitch's wounds. Wordlessly, he bids her to sit back down on the sofa, then disappears into the bathroom to get bandages. Hitchcock shows him moving down the corridor, at the end of which is what appears to be the main door to the house. The director holds this shot as Mitch enters the bathroom, and we see that large chunks of the door are being pecked out by the birds. (This shot was established once, earlier, when Mitch was struggling with the gulls.) The effect was accomplished by building parts of the door out of balsa wood and having crew members knock out bits of it from the other side with hammers and chisels.

Emerging from the bathroom, Mitch sees what is happening and nearly panics. He grabs a tall, antique mirrored coatrack and puts it in front of the door, then begins securing it in place with a hammer and nails. Just as he rejoins the others, there is an extremely loud screech from the birds (once again, very artificial), and suddenly the lights go out. The suggestion is that one or more birds have impacted the power lines, or a transformer, and have been electrocuted.

Proving himself ever resourceful, Mitch immediately grabs a large flashlight from another room, though the living room is still illuminated by the light from the fire. Melanie and Mitch watch in horror as the birds now begin pecking through the side door. Then, just as we have seen before, the attack suddenly . . . stops. The sounds of the birds decrease in number and intensity and begin to fade, suggesting that they are leaving the area.

There follows what is, for me, the most striking series of shots in the entire film—and one of the most impressive sequences in all of Hitchcock's work. We see the ceiling shot from a very low angle. Mitch slowly steps into frame, from the right. "They're going," he says. Then, the ceiling again, from a similar angle. Melanie now steps into view, from the left side of the frame, eyes full of expectation. Then, a third shot of the ceiling, Lydia stepping into view from the right, her eyes scanning the ceiling warily. Finally, the camera slowly tracks back from Lydia to encompass all three actors, their faces illuminated by the glow of the fire.

The ceiling represents the threat from above, from the outside world. That threat has been mostly *suggested* for the last ten minutes; the birds themselves were seen only in Mitch's brief struggle with the gulls at the window. The powerful effect of this sequence of three shots is hard to put into words. "Suspense" is not right, as the suspense is now over: the attack has ended. I can only resort to a word I have probably used too often in this book: we feel we are in the presence of the uncanny. Whenever I watch this sequence of shots, I notice that I have forgotten to breathe. It is cinema artistry at its absolute best.

We now dissolve to much later in the night—near dawn, in fact. There is a closeup of the fire, just as one of the logs burns through and collapses, suggesting it has been a while since the fire was tended to. Then we see a medium shot of Lydia, perfectly framed, sitting on the bench before the piano. She is sound asleep, head drooping, arms in her lap, looking much older than she did earlier in the film. The camera pans to show the rest of the room. Cathy is sleeping on the sofa, curled up under a blanket. Mitch is dozing in an upholstered chair, arm now bandaged. Melanie, however, sits wide awake on the sofa, at Cathy's feet.

Suddenly, she hears the unmistakable sound of wings fluttering. Furthermore, it sounds like it is coming from somewhere inside the house. Melanie looks around, then hears the fluttering again. "Mitch?" she says, gently trying to wake him. But seeing that he is sound asleep, she decides to investigate matters on her own. Melanie takes the large flashlight from the coffee table and switches it on. Thinking that the sound might be the lovebirds, she moves to the kitchen and shines the light into their cage. As Melanie looks at them, sitting perched in the cage and perfectly still, we hear the fluttering once more. She turns, and her flashlight illuminates the stairs to the attic. (We should note that "attic" really refers to the upper floor of the house, which seems to contain more than one bedroom.) As she moves towards the stairs, the suspense mounts: Melanie is now doing exactly what the audience does *not* want her to do.

Hitchcock intercuts shots of Melanie with her point of view, the flashlight casting an eerie bare, white glow on the stairs. We are sure that some horror is to come. The camera now focusses on the door at the top of the stairs. Eyes full of apprehension, Melanie begins to slowly ascend the staircase and to move toward that door. Then she stands before it. She reaches out to turn the knob, then hears fluttering again and hesitates. Melanie turns her head in the direction of the floor below, as if she is considering whether it might be a smarter idea to go and wake Mitch after all. But she decides against it. Melanie slowly turns the knob. She must, she simply *must* see what is on the other side.

Melanie looks up at the door as she slowly pushes it open, her face solemn. She steps in. The room is almost completely dark, but there is a pale light coming from above. With a gasp, Melanie registers the fact that a hole has been torn in the rafters. The sky is exposed, the light of dawn seeping in. Just as she registers this, Melanie steps further into the room and then lifts the flashlight, illuminating a canopied bed—covered in birds.

Immediately, they take flight and hurl themselves toward her. Melanie jumps back, but as she does she impacts the door, shutting herself inside the room. Hundreds of birds, seemingly of all species, now descend upon Melanie Daniels. Hunter's script included a small, eerie detail: the first thing she illuminates with her flashlight is an owl, sitting perched in the room and staring directly at her. It flies at Melanie and strikes her, causing her to fall against the door, slamming it shut. This detail was dropped, for whatever reason, and I can't recall seeing any owls in the film at all.

In the script, the sound of the door slamming shut quickly summons Mitch, who nonetheless has a difficult time getting the door open after Melanie collapses against it. In the film, a great deal more time passes before Mitch arrives on the scene to rescue her. Hitchcock intercuts shots of the birds flying at Melanie, shots of her batting them away, and shots of her hand grasping at the doorknob behind her, trying to escape. The editing here is extremely rapid, with the longest shots lasting a mere three seconds. As the birds relentlessly attack Melanie, her hitherto immaculate green suit (which had not acquired a single wrinkle or stain in three days of wear) is ripped and torn. Her legs and arms are bloodied. In three disturbing shots, birds come dangerously close to Melanie's eyes. We cannot help but think of Dan Fawcett and of Annie.

Some shots clearly involve fake birds, and today's cynical, jaded audiences are likely to infer that the entire thing was fakery. This would be much to Miss Hedren's chagrin, since almost the entire sequence involved real birds, and placed her in considerable danger. Hedren recalled:

The morning we were to start the scene, the assistant director, Jim Brown, came into my dressing room and seemed to be avoiding looking at me. I said, "What's the matter with you?" and he mumbled, "We can't use the mechanical birds." [*N.b.*: Because Hitchcock realized they looked too fake.] I said, "Uh, well, what are we going to use?" He answered, "There's a bunch of ravens and crows." When I walked out on the set, I saw that they had built a huge cage around it—to keep the birds from flying up into the rafters—and inside the set were prop men with big, thick leather gloves up to their elbows to protect themselves from being bitten when they held the birds and hurled them at me.

The scene took a week to film, during which more than 500 birds were hurled at Tippi Hedren. She continues,

By Wednesday of the shooting week, I was tired. By Thursday, I was noticeably nervous. On Friday they had me down on the floor with the birds tied loosely to me with elastic bands, which were attached through the peck-holes in my dress. Well, one of the birds clawed my eye, and that did it; I just sat and cried. It was an incredible physical ordeal. It was very hard for Hitch at this time, too. He wouldn't come out of his office until we were absolutely ready to shoot because he couldn't stand to watch it. I'll never forget the day Cary Grant came on the set during a break from shooting *That Touch of Mink*. He was stunned by what I was going through and said to me, "You're one brave lady." I then considered the possibility that maybe this was one of the reasons why Hitchcock had chosen an unknown for the part—there was an element of danger in it, since the birds were not all nice guys.

After Hedren broke down crying, she went to take a nap in her dressing room. When it proved impossible for the crew to wake her, a doctor was summoned. The diagnosis was nervous exhaustion, and a full week of rest was prescribed. When Hitchcock protested, saying that there was nothing else left to shoot, the doctor responded, "Are you trying to kill her?" Hedren got her week off, then returned to the set to finish what was left of the scene. The entire sequence lasts just over two minutes and while it is masterful, it is two of the most unbearable minutes in the history of film.

Melanie whimpers and cries, but never screams. A large gash appears on her forehead. It seems like all the birds in the world are in that room, attacking her. The sound of their fluttering becomes a roar. After a while, exhausted, Melanie almost ceases trying to fight them off. She gives up her feeble attempts to open the door behind her and slumps against it, then begins sliding down to the floor.

She calls out once, to Mitch, very softly. Then, just before she loses consciousness, she cries, "Get Cathy, and get out of here . . . !" This line is almost inaudible. The subtitles in the version I watched attribute the line to Lydia, but do not actually give the line, referring to it as "indistinct." In the script, Lydia is heard from behind the door speaking to Mitch, saying "Mitch, get her out of there!" But in the film, it is clearly Hedren's voice, and Hedren's mouth is moving; moreover, "Cathy" is distinctly audible.

It is just about when Melanie loses consciousness that we finally hear Mitch at the door. "Melanie! Melanie!" he cries frantically. Mitch tries pushing the door open, but Melanie's unconscious body is firmly wedged against it. He persists, succeeding in rolling her forward a bit, then grabs at her dress, trying to pull her out. Finally, he manages to roll her body a foot or so away from the door, and we see that Lydia is in the corridor behind him.

Immediately, the birds descend upon Mitch. Now he must defend himself *and* try to lift Melanie up at the same time. When he finally succeeds in getting a good grip on her dress, the birds attack his hand without mercy. We see that Lydia is doing her part as well, hitting at the birds as they try to exit the room. Finally, we breathe a great sigh of relief as Mitch succeeds in pulling Melanie out the door and shutting it.

So what are we to make of this strange and harrowing scene? It presents a puzzle for the simple reason that it is *not logical*: there appears to be no logical reason why Melanie goes to that room.

As I noted in chapter six, Hunter included material in his original screenplay that was intended specifically to convey to the audience that Melanie was *not* in any way the cause or focus of the bird attacks. Hitchcock not only deleted this material, but had Hunter insert new dialogue that raised suspicions about Melanie. Specifically, I am referring to the crazed woman's lines in the Tides Restaurant: "They said when you got here the whole thing started. . . . I think you're the cause of all this."

But *how* exactly could Melanie be the focus or "cause" of all this? Hunter sarcastically suggested that Hitchcock left the audience to imagine that "what happened . . . may have been an isolated experience brought on by God knows what—Melanie's flighty earlier days? Lydia's rejection of her? Who knows?" I submit that this suggestion actually deserves to be taken seriously.

In an earlier chapter, I noted that *The Birds* prominently features dysfunctional, modern relationships between men and women, and parents and children. Melanie's mother "ditched" her when she was eleven (note that Cathy turns eleven in the film). Is this the reason that she spends her time on mischief, jumping into fountains and playing destructive practical jokes? Mitch certainly thinks it may be, when he half-jokingly says to her, "You need a mother's care, my child." (This remark precipitates the revelation about Melanie's mother.)

Certainly, her status as a child of affluence has only made matters worse. She is, in every way, a modern woman: spoiled, entitled, unserious, self-involved, vain, cosmopolitan, deracinated ("we're sending a little Korean boy through school"), and trivial. She is also a feminist of sorts: it is she who pursues Mitch, and not the other way around.

Like a female bird with gender dysphoria, Melanie comes to Bodega Bay and does a little mating dance outside the Oedipal nest Mitch has made with his mother and is unable to leave. Because of his mother's jealousy, he cannot make a real connection with another woman. Both mother and son are made perverse by this relationship. He is unable to grow as a man, and she becomes the "anti-mother," placing her own needs above those of her son. Mitch calls his mother "dear" and "darling," as a husband would. Cathy is a bit of a brat (though Camille Paglia despises her as sugar and spice and everything nice). Cathy sasses her mother ("I know all that democracy jazz") and seems to be seeking something from Melanie that Lydia cannot give her.

As noted in chapter three, the development of these characters has been arrested; they play the wrong roles, or roles have been reversed. They are, in a word, *unnatural*. Thus, nature enters, in the form of the birds, to "realign" these lives. *In this process, Melanie is absolutely central.* The Mitch-Lydia relationship can only be put right by a woman whose need of Mitch is so absolute that Lydia simply must release him.

But this cannot occur until Melanie abandons all her guile, her malignant mischief, and, especially, her "feminist" independence. Then Mitch, who had initially seemed like *he* needed saving, can save her. And it is only if Melanie can release herself in this way that she herself can grow and be healed. In effect, she must return to being the helpless eleven-year-old girl abandoned by her mother. This is what is accomplished by her encounter with the birds in the attic. (In the next chapter, I will say more about how the encounter changes Lydia and transforms her relationship with Melanie.)

In Hunter's original script, Melanie goes up the stairs and heads straight for that one door, just as she does in the finished film. In his story conferences with Hunter, however, Hitchcock pressed the writer on exactly why Melanie does this. Years later, Hunter recalled:

> I had her going up to the attic after she heard a bird peeping. Hitch asked, "If she hears birds in the house, why doesn't she wake Mitch?" I said, "Because she's not sure there are birds in the house." Hitch persisted. "But if she thinks there are birds in that room, why would she open the door?" I had no answer. He said, "All right, it's a good scene, but let's take the curse off it. Let's have her open a lot of doors and find no birds anyplace and therefore opens the last door believing it's safe to do so."[3]

Even though the pair agreed to this change, and it was incorporated into the script, when it came time to shoot the scene Hitchcock reverted to Hunter's original idea: Melanie opens only one door, the one that has the birds behind it. Hedren apparently also did not understand why Melanie opens that door. When she asked Hitchcock why Melanie does this, according to legend he responded, "Because I tell you to."

Yes, there is no logical answer to why Melanie acts as she does, and Hitchcock was right to press Hunter on this.

---

[3] Counts and Rubin, "The Making of Alfred Hitchcock's *The Birds*."

In the end, however, he realized that the attack on Melanie was necessary to provide a climax to the film, one which would provide a *psychological* resolution to the problems of these characters. This was doubly necessary because, in fact, it is the *only* resolution provided by the film.

By having Melanie go up the stairs and open only that one door, Hitchcock suggests that there is an *inevitability* to her final encounter with the birds. Note how Hitchcock's camera focusses on that door, and *only* that door, as Melanie ascends the stairs. He intercuts shots of Melanie moving up the stairs with her point of view, moving *us*, the audience, closer and closer to the door. We are left with the sense that this encounter *had* to come; that there had to come a moment when Melanie, and only Melanie, confronted the birds.

In the end, it is hard to escape the impression that Melanie has *offered herself* to the birds, in an act of self-sacrifice—one which, as I have said, in the end "puts right" all of the characters, including herself.[4] We have already seen one act of self-sacrifice by a character in the film: Annie redeems herself by saving Cathy from the birds, at the cost of her own life. That Melanie's act is also a form of self-sacrifice, that she has overcome her frivolous egocentrism, is underscored by the insertion of her line "Get Cathy, and get out of here" as she slumps to the floor, unconscious.

You see, it *really was* all about Melanie from the very beginning. The crazed woman was right when she said, "I

---

[4] Hunter's original script made it clear that Melanie deliberately shuts herself inside the attic to stop the birds from penetrating further into the house. In the film, it is not clear that she shuts the door deliberately. Hitchcock described Melanie's actions as "self-sacrificial." See Moral, *The Making of Hitchcock's* The Birds, 138.

think you're the cause of all this." Such a claim would have incensed the literal-minded Evan Hunter. But Melanie is not the "cause" in any literal or logical sense. This is a film in which what happens can only be understood in terms of psychology, and metaphysics.

I have offered the psychological explanation, so what of metaphysics? Here we must recognize that the film operates on multiple levels. On one level, Melanie's encounter with the birds brings about a psychological resolution. But keep in mind that I have argued that the characters in the film represent modernity, or modern "types." And here I do not have in mind only Melanie, Annie, and the Brenners, but also the other significant characters in the film, especially Mrs. Bundy. As we have seen, Hitchcock stated on more than one occasion that the theme of the film is "complacency." I have argued in this book that the film depicts an encounter between complacent, modern man and the uncanny. The bird attacks represent the arrival of a Heideggerian Event: a fundamental shift in the meaning, or being of things. As I discussed in chapter four, for Heidegger we do not control such "events"; we do not make them happen, they happen to us.

Ultimately, the origins of meaning/being are mysterious. But this is, of course, an affront to the mentality of modern man. We believe that we have laid bare the meaning of things, and have tamed the surrounding world, which we conceptualize as raw material for the satisfaction of our desires. The coming of the birds is a rebuke to that modern hubris—and a complete overturning of the world we thought we had built. Initially, modern man, speaking through Mrs. Bundy, declares all of this "impossible," "ridiculous," "unimaginable," on the basis of something we called "logic," but that suddenly seems no longer to function. In the face of this great unknown, when it manifests itself (always manifesting, as Heidegger might say, *in its essential hiddenness*) we have two choices. We can try, for a while, to deny mystery, to deny the intrinsic hiddenness of being, as Mrs. Bundy does (until she is stunned into repentant silence); or we can surrender to mystery. This is what Melanie does when she enters that dark room in the attic. This is the metaphysical meaning of *The Birds*.

But there is one further element that may be in play in this climactic confrontation. As I have mentioned several times already, blindness is a theme that comes up repeatedly in the film, even (indirectly) in Annie's reference to Oedipus. This is one of the most frightening aspects of *The Birds*. It is hard to imagine anything more awful than being blinded. As fates worse than death, it is right up there with castration. The film puts us in fear of blindness early on when Mitch tells the others "Cover your eyes!" as the birds rush down the chimney and into the Brenner living room. Then, in possibly the most grisly scene in any Hitchcock film, Farmer Fawcett is found blinded. Then Annie is blinded. Three times in the attic scene, Hitchcock's camera shows Hedren in closeup, with wide open eyes as birds come dangerously near those beautiful eyes. Once, the camera shows us Melanie's point of view, and a bird flies directly into the lens, as if flying into Melanie's eyes.

I argued in chapter five that the real "blindness" showcased in the film is the blindness of modern human beings relentlessly pursuing their desire to "see": to know, to make all that exists fully transparent and manipulable. Tiresias warns Oedipus to give up his quest to find his father's murderer, because some things are best *not known*. But Oedipus persists, with devastating consequences. His real blindness is much like the blindness of modern man: not perceiving the limits of knowledge, or the unintended consequences of its relentless pursuit. In *The Birds*, this blindness is principally represented by Mrs. Bundy. But we see it in the other characters as well. Lydia is compelled,

against her better judgment, to move down the dark corridor in Dan Fawcett's house and to make her traumatic
discovery of his body—compelled by her irresistible desire
to see. And could this also be the reason Melanie climbs
those stairs to the attic?

As I put it earlier, Melanie must, she simply *must* see
what is on the other side of that door. The situation is
mythic—she is become Pandora, or Bluebeard's last wife.
What does she find on the other side? The revelation—
the apocalypse. The opening of a new vision; a fundamental shift in the meaning of things; a hubris-crushing
Heideggerian Event. In surrendering to the great unknown—the great abyss beyond human reason, from
which spring *all* the "events," all the epochs of being—
the eyes of Melanie Daniels' soul are opened for the first
time, as the birds relentlessly pursue the stubbornly unseeing eyes in her head. As Tiresias says of Oedipus, she
had eyes, but she did not see.

But for now we must end this metaphysical reverie and
return to our story, for there is more to be learned here.

CHAPTER NINE

Mitch gathers Melanie's still unconscious body into his arms and carries her down the stairs. Lydia walks ahead of him, carrying an oil lamp. "Oh, poor thing! Poor thing!" she says. Her resentment toward Melanie now completely gone, she feels only pity. Lydia goes to fetch bandages as Mitch lays Melanie on the living room sofa. He asks Cathy to get some brandy, and the little girl brings over a bottle and a glass. Mitch now examines Melanie's wounds in the light and grimaces. The gash on her forehead appears deep and there are cuts on both her cheeks.

Suddenly, Melanie opens her eyes wide and begins frantically clawing the air. She does not see Mitch, or that her surroundings have changed. She is still fighting the birds. Mitch grabs her arms, which are also covered in cuts and scratches. "No, no. It's all right. It's all right," he says, soothingly, and presses her arms onto her chest. Cathy is overcome with emotion and turns away, crying quietly. Mitch tries to get Melanie to sip some brandy, but her lips do not move, and she looks away from him, not looking at anything in particular, seeing nothing. She just lies there, catatonic, arms crossed over her chest like a corpse.

Lydia enters with water, antiseptic, and bandages. She and Mitch then begin cleaning and dressing Melanie's wounds. At this point, the screenplay contains some small but significant differences from the completed film. First of all, Mitch begins unrolling bandages, but his hands are trembling, and he drops the roll. "Let me do that, Mitch," Lydia says gently. "I can handle it," he insists. He doesn't want to be treated like a little boy. With emphasis, Lydia responds, "I know you can." Hunter specifies that "her eyes meet his," and she says, "But I'd like to." Here, two things are happening. She is affirming that he is a man, but also signaling her desire to care for Melanie.

Furthermore, in the screenplay Melanie speaks, though she is somewhat delirious. "Please don't mess me up with bandages, Mrs. Brenner," she says, and Lydia shushes her. Melanie continues to talk for the rest of the screenplay and is not depicted as catatonic. In the film, she remains in a stupor, aside from uttering two words, as we shall see. Hitchcock's changes to Hunter's script emphasize Melanie's complete helplessness and reduction to an infantile state.

In the film, and in the screenplay, Mitch insists that they must get Melanie to a hospital. His plan is to head for San Francisco. Lydia doubts that they will make it, but Mitch insists that they must try. "I'm frightened, terribly frightened," Lydia says. "I don't know what's outside there." In the screenplay, Mitch responds, "What do we have to know, Mother? We're all together, we all love each other, we all need each other. What else is there? Mother, I want us to stay alive!"

It's a melodramatic line and was rightfully cut, but Lydia's response (again, only in the screenplay) is interesting. She nods and says, "I started to say . . . inside . . ." What does this mean? She had said a moment earlier "I don't know what's outside there." The line is slightly different in the script, and Lydia hesitates at the beginning of it: "I . . . I don't know what's out there." Does she mean that she had started to say, "I don't know what's *inside* there"? Inside where? In the screenplay, Mitch holds out his hand to her and says, "You don't have to." Was Lydia about to commit a Freudian slip? Was she about to confess that she is afraid of what's happening in the house, between Mitch and Melanie? Or does she not know what is inside herself, inside her heart, perhaps? This is true—but in the end, she finds out.

Throughout this book, I have included discussion of

the differences between the screenplay and the film because those differences shed light on the film's meaning. Hitchcock's changes to the screenplay often give us important clues to the director's intentions and what he thought the point of the film was. In almost every case, Hitchcock's changes improve the story and give it depth. Hunter's dialogue is sometimes flabby and melodramatic, and Hitchcock pruned it quite intelligently.

However, there is material that was cut from the script that sometimes sheds more light on the characters and their motivations, and sometimes one wishes that it had been left in. As I have demonstrated here, this is particularly true with some of the dialogue between Mitch and Lydia. The troubled nature of this mother-son relationship is clearer in the screenplay than it is in the finished film.

In any case, Mitch decides that they will take Melanie's Aston Martin, because it will be faster than their pickup truck. This is a somewhat strange decision, since Melanie's car is a convertible with a canopy that could easily be torn to pieces by the birds—but we'll find out the real reason for this in a moment, and it has to do with Hunter's original, planned ending to the film. It only took about two dozen viewings of this film over the years for me to remember that Mitch was seen with a car earlier. It was a 1962 Ford Galaxie 500 Town Victoria 75A—a four-door sedan with a hard top. Why not use that car? It would be faster than the truck and more secure than the Aston Martin. Did Mitch leave it at the Tides when he went to meet Melanie? We'll never know.

Mitch heads to the front door, intending to get Melanie's car out of the garage and bring it around. Lydia says, "Mitch, see if you can get anything on the car radio." Hitchcock then shows us the exterior of the Brenner's front door, in closeup. It is covered in scratches and gouges. The door opens and Mitch moves into view. As he looks at the front yard, his face takes on an expression of horror. Then we see his point of view: birds cover the entire earth, or at least it looks that way. Birds cover the ground and are perched on every object within sight. Part of the image is another matte painting by Albert Whitlock. It shows sunlight streaming through the clouds in the distance, which some have interpreted as a sign of hope.

Some of the birds in the shot are real, and we can see them moving. Some are fake (it is safe to assume in this film that anytime a bird is not moving it is a stuffed prop or a cardboard cutout). The real birds were, in some cases, tied to the objects they perch on, via cords placed around their talons. Some were drugged. And some were actually chickens and ducks (sometimes with dyed plumage), though these were placed in the background. Paul Ridge, a representative of the American Humane Association, was always on set to make sure that the birds were well-treated. He reported no problems. Bird trainer Ray Berwick seems to have been very fond of his charges and kept some as pets.[1]

Mitch swallows hard and slowly moves out onto the porch. Gulls surround his feet. Indeed, he must inch forward as gently as possible, as the ground is covered in hundreds of birds. Needless to say, he is desperate not to excite them. As he begins to descend the steps, he reaches out to touch the wooden railing. Several ravens are perched there and one of them caws loudly and gives his hand a nasty peck. This particular raven was the aptly named Nosey, Berwick's pet. In order to produce this reaction from Nosey, Rod Taylor's hand was smeared with

---

[1] Tony Lee Moral reports that "In total, 25,000 birds were used in the film, 3,000 birds trained, with 30 specials [sic? "species"?], 2,000 finches, 700 English sparrows, 500 ducks and 125 ravens. The gulls and assorted larger birds consumed 100 pounds of shrimp, anchovies and ground meat per week." See Moral, *The Making of Hitchcock's* The Birds, 104.

meat. (Some descriptions of this scene identify Nosey as a crow, but he looks like a raven to me; Berwick said years later, "Pound for pound, I think the raven and cockatoo are the most intelligent beings on earth.")

Despite the presence of countless winged mankillers, an eerie calm prevails. This is heightened by the sound effects, which play quietly in the background. We hear wings fluttering softly and little cooing and cawing noises. Behind these, however, there is what sounds like the rush of wind, though it is eerie and artificial. A similar sound effect accompanies the "God's eye view" shot of Bodega Bay, as the gulls mass for their attack, discussed extensively in chapter six. According to Tony Lee Moral, Hitchcock asked for "an electronic silence" that might suggest the mental state of the birds. "There should be a monotony," the director said. "'Like the distant roar of the sea.' But it should be strange, it should say, 'we're not ready to start yet, we're getting ready, we're like an engine that is purring, but we haven't started off yet.'"[2]

Mitch succeeds in making it to the side door of the garage, even as gulls nip at his pant legs. He enters the structure, which is not attached to the house, and is about to try and open the garage door when he remembers Lydia's request that he listen to the car radio. He gets into Melanie's car and turns the radio on, then locates a station with news on Bodega Bay. The announcer is in the middle of reading the story:

> . . . The bird attacks have subsided for the time being. Bodega Bay seems to be the center, though there are reports of minor attacks on Sebastopol and a few on Santa Rosa. Bodega Bay has been cordoned off by roadblocks. Most of the townspeople have managed to get out, but there are still some

---

[2] Moral, *The Making of Hitchcock's* The Birds, 165.

isolated pockets of people. No decision has been arrived at yet as to what the next step will be, but there's been some discussion as to whether the military should go in. It appears that the bird attacks come in waves with long intervals between. The reason for this does not seem clear as yet.

Nor will it ever be clear.

Mitch switches off the radio, gets out, and then very carefully opens the garage door. He returns to the car, starts it, and then allows the vehicle to roll ever so slowly out of the garage and up to the front door. The car moves through a veritable sea of gulls, and Mitch is trying desperately hard not to crush any of them. He carefully gets out of the car and then slowly moves up the front steps, wading through more gulls. Finally, he manages to slip back into the house, quickly shutting the door behind him. For those seeing the film for the first time (and even multiple times), the suspense in this scene is agonizing.

Inside the house, Lydia sits on the couch, holding Melanie close. She wears a brown overcoat and has helped Melanie into her mink. The authors of *Cinemafantastique*'s 1980 article on the making of the film comment, correctly, that the mink is "now a hollow reminder of her status, a privileged position which has failed to protect her from the wrath of the birds."[3] Melanie's head is now bandaged, with a thin diagonal line of blood seeping through the gauze. The cuts on her cheeks also seem to still be bleeding. Her hands and wrists are also bandaged. She stares straight ahead, her expression completely vacant. Cathy stands over her, putting on her own little coat, studying Melanie with a mixture of fear and incomprehension.

Mitch and Lydia now help Melanie up and, supporting

---

[3] Counts and Rubin, "The Making of Alfred Hitchcock's *The Birds*."

her, they move toward the front door. The camera holds a medium shot of Mitch, Melanie, and Lydia, tracking backward and into the darkest part of the room. The trio are enveloped in shadow. Then we see Mitch reach his hand downward and out of frame. We hear the doorknob turning. Mitch's arm sweeps back toward his body, opening the door and illuminating the three characters with the morning light.

I have described these actions in detail because this is actually one of the most remarkable shots in the film. Most viewers will not realize, even on repeat viewings, *that there is actually no door*. And there could not be—otherwise the camera could not have photographed the trio. The entire effect was accomplished with lighting, plus Rod Taylor pantomiming opening the door. The shot has been referred to as Hitchcock's "magic door trick." He employed a similar technique in 1950's *Stage Fright*.

We now see their point of view: the convertible sitting in front of the house, surrounded by birds. If anything, there now seem to be more birds in the yard than there were before. As Mitch and Lydia lead Melanie out, the latter suddenly wakes up from her stupor. She looks around at the birds, eyes wild, and then cries "No. No!" They are the last words she will utter in the film. Mitch and Lydia manage to calm her, and as the three move down the steps and toward the car, Hitchcock intercuts shots of Lydia and Melanie, both of them terrified. The ravens are seen again on the railing, this time cawing sharply. Are the birds about to attack?

Finally, they reach the car. Mitch opens the passenger side door and helps his mother and Melanie into the back seat. Cathy now calls to him from the front porch, the caged lovebirds at her feet.[4] "Can I bring the lovebirds,

---

[4] During the making of the film, the cast and crew threw a thirteenth birthday party for Veronica Cartwright, complete

Mitch?" she says hesitantly. "They haven't harmed any-one." "All right, bring them," he responds. This always elicits from me a groan or at least a smirk.

Commentators have interpreted this small touch as a sign of "hope" at the film's end. Actually, its inclusion is deeply pessimistic. Hitchcock is promising us that the human foolishness will continue. Cathy is like the little child in Isaiah (see chapter seven): "The wolf also shall dwell with the lamb, the leopard shall lie down with the young goat, the calf and the young lion and the fatling together; and a little child shall lead them." No, actually, it won't be that way. But we never learn.

Cathy picks up the birdcage, and Mitch helps her into the front passenger seat. In the back, we see that Melanie is huddled against Lydia. The older woman looks down when she realizes that Melanie is grasping her wrist tight-ly. Melanie looks up at her, with an expression that con-veys, all at once, pain, fear, and something else. Is it love? The Melanie we met at the beginning of the film seems to be gone. She now seems as innocent as a child—and that is, indeed, what she has been reduced to. Lydia looks back at her, for the first time, with real affection. With love, even. She presses her head against Melanie's. It is a touch-ing moment, beautifully photographed.

In this moment, which lasts just twelve seconds, sever-al things have happened that are of great significance for our characters. The first and most obvious is that Lydia has accepted Melanie. In doing so, further, she releases Mitch; she relinquishes her control over him. This is tan-tamount to overcoming her fear of abandonment—by means of abandoning herself, and her selfish desire to hold onto her son. She now accepts Mitch not as a substi-tute husband, but as a son and as a man, who can and will and *must* leave her.

---

with cake and gifts. Tippi Hedren gave her lovebirds.

But Melanie too is changed in this moment. She overcomes her own abandonment through a surrogate mother figure. She is born again. No longer frivolous, spiteful, and duplicitous, she has been changed by her commitment to this family—a largely unchosen commitment, that has blossomed into love. The birds have freed her to become who she really is. She could not do this on her own.

As to Mitch, he has achieved, by this point, a kind of masculine apotheosis. In primal conflict with nature, he has risen to the occasion as a man and protected the women. His mother has finally released him, and he has another to care for—someone with whom, we sense, he will begin a new life. Not "when all of this is over," but *now*. For "all of this" is never over. Life continues amidst adversity.

As to Cathy, her own story and character are not of great importance here, but we can see that she has been strengthened through the addition of Melanie to the family.

Mitch starts the car. Immediately, the birds begin cawing and squawking angrily. The car moves forward. Then we see the same shot of the yard shown a few minutes ago, the one partially accomplished with a matte painting. Slowly, the car moves through the yard, off the property, and onto the road, as the sound of the birds becomes louder and more ominous. As the car advances down the road, it picks up speed. It continues to move far away from us, then we see it round a bend. Just as the car almost completely disappears from view, the picture fades quickly to black. There is a pause, and then a simple title card ends the film: "A Universal Release." The words are superimposed over a stylized globe, in the same color scheme established in the opening credits. The final shot of the film lasts twenty-seven seconds but took three months to complete. It is a composite shot, involving not only Whitlock's matte painting but also thirty-two different exposures. Hitchcock described it as "the most difficult single shot I've ever done."

So that's it. The End. Or is it? *The Birds* certainly has an unconventional ending, and this is one of the things about it that I love the most. Aside from the psychological resolution to the characters and their relationships, there is no resolution to the story, and no explanation of why the birds behaved as they did. Had Hitchcock ended the film in a more conventional way, both its impact and its subsequent reputation as a "great film" would have been considerably diminished. Indeed, the inclusion of a resolution or explanation would have completely negated what I have argued is the film's meaning.

In 1963, audiences reacted negatively to the ending. "Was that it?" some were heard to say. Others, as *Cinemafantastique* notes, "expecting answers to the questions posed by the film, misinterpreted the blank screen as a break in the reel. To avoid confusion come release-time, [assistant editor] Bud Hoffman had Technicolor do an overlay clearly announcing that it was, in fact, 'THE END.' As it was too late to add the title to the original negative, the title had to be overlay printed on every existing copy of the film." This was, moreover, at the insistence of the studio. Thankfully, copies in circulation today (available on home video, for example) do not include this.

American audiences in 1963 were, it would seem, almost as dim as audiences today. They wanted a happy ending—or at least a definite one. And they wanted pat answers. Many of them would probably have characterized themselves, ironically, as "mystery lovers." The truth is that they could not tolerate mystery. In short, they were a modern audience, meaning an audience shaped by modernity. They didn't get that they were all Mrs. Bundy, and that *The Birds* is rebuking *them*.

Audiences then and now are unaware that this was *not* how *The Birds* was originally supposed to end. After the

Brenners and Melanie drive away from the farm, Hunter's screenplay, even in later drafts, goes on for another seven pages. I will not summarize the events in detail, aside from saying that Hunter has them driving through Bodega Bay, witnessing the aftermath of widespread carnage. Windows are broken, cars are overturned, and there are several dead bodies. Perhaps the best detail in the sequence is a dead man seen on the side of the road "clutching a television set in his arms."

And everywhere, the birds are perched. When the car reaches the highway, Mitch really floors it. "Here we go," he says. The birds immediately take flight, pursuing the car. They begin to divebomb the vehicle's soft canopy, ripping holes in it. The women become hysterical. The most dramatic moment comes when Lydia cries out at the sky: "'Dear God . . . dear God . . . please, please, what have we done? Please.' (and then in anger at the roof and the birds) 'Can't they leave us alone?' (shrieking it) 'LEAVE US ALONE!'" Eventually, the car begins to outdistance the birds. "We're losing them," Lydia says, calming down. The final line of the script belongs to Mitch: "It looks clear up ahead." Hunter then specifies, "FULL SHOT—THE CAR moving AWAY FROM THE CAMERA FAST into magnificent sunrise over the crest of the hills. Further and further into the distance it goes. FADE OUT: THE END" Hurrah! Our heroes are safe, riding off into a hopeful sunrise.[5]

Ho hum.

Only part of this projected sequence was filmed. After

---

[5] Hitchcock also planned at one point for Melanie to scream "Let me out, let me go back! Mother, I want you, I want you. Come back to me, please, please come back to me." This would have resolved the mother issue raised earlier in the film—by making it far too clumsy and explicit. Thankfully, the idea was dropped. The "resolution" presented in the finished film is far more effective. See Moral, *The Making of Hitchcock's The Birds*, 54.

location work, Hitchcock returned to Los Angeles to begin
shooting in the studio. Robert Boyle and Albert Whitlock,
among others, were still in Bodega Bay, and Hitchcock
asked them to shoot the footage showing the Aston Martin driving through the devastated town. The men covered
the road in debris, smeared buildings with ketchup (simu-
lating blood), and laid a large quantity of dead chickens
around town (acquired from a butcher). When the repre-
sentatives of Animal Protection showed up to observe
filming, they assumed that the crew had slaughtered the
chickens, and one of them became violent, tearing Boyle's
clothing![6]

In the end, however, Hitchcock decided not to use any
of this footage, or to shoot the rest of what Hunter had
scripted. Years later, he explained his decision: "I excluded
those scenes because I felt they were superfluous. Emotionally speaking, the movie was already over for the audience. The additional scenes would have been playing
while everyone was leaving their seats and walking up the
aisles. We used to call these hat-feeling scenes."

This last comment refers to how, when audiences
begin feeling that a film has gone on too long, they get
antsy and begin feeling the brims of the hats they hold in
their laps, waiting for the credits so that they can get up
and leave. At least, in the days when people still wore hats
(or took them off).

Even decades later, Hunter was bitter about Hitchcock's decision to cut these scenes. Apparently, the entire
reason his script specified that Melanie drives a convertible was to make possible the drama of his final scene,
when the car's canopy is ripped by the birds. In an interview from 1980 (partially quoted in the last chapter),
Hunter said "I don't feel the new ending is ambiguous. I
feel it is simply puzzling. With such a large question

---

[6] See Moral, *The Making of Hitchcock's* The Birds, 144.

looming, it seems to me the end of the film should have at least been decisive." Hunter was a talented writer, but he was fundamentally conventional. He wanted a "decisive" ending and definite answers. Somewhere along the way, Hitchcock decided he wanted ambiguity and no definite answers.

Kyle Counts and Steve Rubin offer a perceptive response to Hunter:

> Actually, it is only after you have seen the film a few times that Hitchcock's ending seems, if not complete, then at least artistically correct. While certainly puzzling, the ambiguity of the final shot may be seen as a thematic element of the film, that facile endings are often misleading in their attempts to pacify audiences. Perhaps more birds will be waiting in San Francisco; or we may assume that what is happening in Bodega Bay—with reports of scattered attacks in the nearby communities of Santa Rosa and Sebastopol—is part of an isolated occurrence, rather than one of world-wide proportions, as du Maurier's story seems to indicate. Infinitely more valuable than any pellucid denouement *The Birds* might have offered is the thought that lingers after its final images have faded.[7]

Indeed. And, as I have argued (persuasively, I hope), Hitchcock's changes to Hunter's script were motivated, in part, by the desire to make the audience think. By ending the film without any real resolution or explanations, he is signaling his belief that the world is deeply mysterious, far more mysterious than we moderns are willing to admit; that full and final explanations are not forthcoming, nor

---

[7] Counts and Rubin, "The Making of Alfred Hitchcock's *The Birds*."

will they be; and that we are *not* the masters of our own fate. This is a far more unsettling film than *Psycho*, which actually featured a definite conclusion as well as a facile psychological explanation for why Norman Bates acted as he did.

The Birds is more unsettling because we know, deep down, that what it is telling us about ourselves is true; that beneath the thin veneer of Progress, there is unfathomable mystery and unspeakable horror. We do not like this; we do not want to be reminded of our vulnerability. That the audience resists the film's conclusion underscores how appropriate and necessary that conclusion is.

* * *

Camille Paglia is quite correct when she notes that "The more microscopically this film is studied, the more it reveals."[8]

But could all these "Heideggerian" layers of meaning really be present in *The Birds*? After all, it is unlikely that Hitchcock ever read Heidegger. Alhough there is a demonstrable "existentialist" influence on *The Birds*, the best answer to this objection is that it is irrelevant. I never claimed that Hitchcock, or Evan Hunter, intended to inject Heideggerian philosophy into the film. I merely claimed that Heidegger's philosophy provides us with a powerful tool for interpreting it.

Interpreting a work of fiction is not merely a matter of identifying its authors' conscious intentions. In fact, that is not even the primary concern. Works of art mean more than their authors intend. Heidegger argues that the meaning of things changes over time. This includes the meaning of films. If *The Birds* now means more to you than it did before, this book has been a success.

---

[8] Paglia, *The Birds*, 2.

INDEX

ABOUT THE AUTHOR

Derek Hawthorne is a philosopher and film critic. He spends part of each year in Bodega Bay, California, the location of *The Birds*. This is his first book.

www.ingramcontent.com/pod-product-compliance
Lightning Source LLC
Chambersburg PA
CBHW020332100426
42812CB00029B/3101/J